YOU
FOREVER

YOU
FOREVER

T. LOBSANG RAMPA

SAMUEL WEISER, INC.

York Beach, Maine

First published in 1990 by
Samuel Weiser, Inc.
Box 612
York Beach, ME 03910

Third printing, 1992

Library of Congress Cataloging-in-Publication Data

Lobsang, Rampa, T. (Tuesday)
    You Forever / T. Lobsang Rampa.
    1. Parapsychology—Research. I. Title.
    BF1031.L64 1990
    131--dc20   90-40257
                                                  CIP

ISBN 0-87728-717-1
MV

Cover painting, "The Closing Ritual," Copyright © 1990 Rob
Schouten. Used by kind permission of the artist.

Printed in the United States of America

The paper used in this publication meets the minimum require-
ments of the American National Standard for Permanence of
Paper for Printed Library Materials Z39.48-1984.

Table of Contents

T. Lobsang Rampa

Foreword

This is a very special course of instruction for those who are sincerely interested in knowing the things which have to be known. At first it was intended that this should be done in the form of a correspondence course, but then it was realized that with all the organization necessary each student would have to pay a huge fee for the course! So, with the cooperation of my publishers, it was decided to produce this material in book form.

You will appreciate that normally in a correspondence course there would be certain questions which a student would want to ask, but I cannot undertake to answer questions arising from this book.

I tell you emphatically that if you read this book you will derive much benefit from it; if you study this book you will derive much more benefit from it. To help you, you will find the instructions included which would have gone out with the correspondence course.

—T. Lobsang Rampa

Instructions

We—you and us—are going to have to work together so that your psychic development may proceed apace. Some of these lessons will be longer and possibly more difficult than others, but these lessons are not padded; they contain, so far as we are able, real meat without fancy trimmings.

Select a definite night each week on which to study each lesson. Get into the habit of studying at a certain time, at a certain place, at a certain day. There is more to it than just reading words because you have to absorb ideas which may be very strange to you, and the mental discipline of regular habits will assist you enormously.

Have some place—some room set aside—where you can be comfortable. You will learn more easily if you are comfortable. Lie down if you prefer, but in any case adopt an attitude where there is no strain upon muscles, where you can relax so that the whole of your attention may be given to the printed words and the thoughts behind them. If you are tensed up, much of your awareness is devoted to sensing the feeling of tenseness! You want to make sure that for an hour, or two hours, or however long it takes you to read the lesson, no one will intrude upon you and break your trend of thought.

In your room—your study—shut the door. Lock it, for preference, and draw close the blinds so that the fluctuations of daylight do not distract your attention. Have just one light on in the room, and that should be a reading lamp placed slightly behind you. This will provide adequate illumination while leaving the rest of the room in suitable shade.

Lie down or adopt any position which is quite comfortable and restful. Relax for a few moments, let yourself breathe deeply, that is, take perhaps three really deep breaths one after the other. Hold the breath for three or four seconds, then let it out over a period of three or four seconds. Rest quietly for a few more seconds, and then pick up the lesson and read it. First read it easily—just work through it as if you were reading the newspaper. When you have done that, pause for a few moments to let what you have so lightly read sink into your subconscious. Then start all over again. Go through the lesson meticulously, paragraph by paragraph. If anything puzzles you, make a note of it, write it down in a conveniently placed notebook. Do not try to memorize anything, there is no point in being a slave to the printed word, the whole purpose of lesson-work such as this is to sink into your subconscious. A conscious attempt to memorize often blinds one to the full meaning of the words. You are not entering into an examination where parrot-like repetition of certain phrases is all that is required. You are, instead, storing up knowledge which can set you free from the bonds of the flesh and enable you to see what manner of thing this human body is, and determine the purpose of life on Earth.

When you have gone through the lesson again, consult your notes and ponder over the points which puzzle you, the points which are not clear to you. It is too easy to just write in to us and have a question answered; that will not cause it to sink into your subconscious. It is kinder and better for you that you should think of the answer yourself.

You must do your part. Anything that is worth having is worth working for. Things which are given away, free, are usually so given because they are not worth charging for! You must open your mind; you must be willing to absorb new knowledge. You must imagine that knowledge is flowing into you. Remember, "As a man thinketh, so is he."

Lesson One

BEFORE WE ATTEMPT to understand the nature of the over-self or deal with any esoteric matters, we must be sure that first we comprehend the nature of humanity. In this course we shall use the term "we" to indicate humanity—both male and female. It is an ongoing problem with the English language that we have no good non-sexist pronoun to indicate the singular individual. Therefore, in some places it has been impossible to avoid the use of "he" or "him"—especially in places where we are discussing general examples of human behavior. Let's at the outset state definitely that woman is the equal of man in all matters—including those relating to the esoteric and extrasensory realms. Women, in fact, often have brighter auras and a greater capacity for appreciation of the various facets of metaphysics. Now, on with our study!

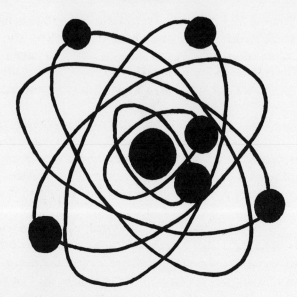

Figure 1. Carbon atom.

Figure 2. The solar system.

What is life? Actually, everything that exists is life. Even a creature which we normally term dead is alive. The normal form of its life may have ceased—as it would have done for us to term it dead—but with the cessation of that life a fresh form of life took over. The process of dissolution creates life of its own.

Everything that is vibrates. Everything consists of molecules in constant motion. We will use molecules instead of atoms, neutrons, protons, etc., because this is a course on metaphysics, not a course of chemistry or physics. We are trying to paint a general picture rather than go into microscopic detail on irrelevant matters.

Perhaps we should say a few words about molecules and atoms first in order to appease the purists who otherwise would write in and give us knowledge which we already possess. Molecules are small, very small, but they can be seen by the use of the electron microscope and by those who are trained in metaphysical arts. According to the dictionary, a molecule is the smallest portion of a substance capable of independent existence while retaining the properties of that substance. Small though molecules are, they are composed of even smaller particles known as atoms.

An atom is like a miniature solar system. The nucleus of the atom represents the Sun in our own solar system. Around this Sun rotate electrons in much the same way as our solar system planets revolve around our Sun. As in the solar system, the atom unit is mostly empty space. Here, in figure 1, is how the carbon atom—the brick of our own Universe—appears when greatly magnified. Figure 2 shows our solar system. Every substance has a different number of electrons around its nucleus "Sun." Uranium, for example, has ninety-two electrons. Carbon has only six. Two close to the nucleus, and four orbiting at a greater distance. But we are going to forget about atoms and refer only to *molecules. ...*

We are a mass of rapidly rotating molecules. We appear to be solid; it is not easy to push a finger through flesh and bone. Yet this solidity is an illusion forced upon us because we, too, are mankind. Consider a creature of infinite smallness who can stand at a distance from a human body and look at it. The creature would see whirling suns, spiral nebulae, and streams akin to the Milky Way. In the soft parts of the body— the flesh—the molecules would be widely dispersed. In the hard substances, the bones, the molecules would be dense, bunched together and giving the appearance of a great cluster of stars.

Imagine yourself standing on the top of a mountain on some clear night. You are alone, far from the lights of any city which, reflecting into the night sky, causes refraction from suspended moisture-drops and makes the heavens appear dim. (This is why observatories are always built in remote districts.) You are on your own mountaintop . . . above you the stars shine clear and brilliant. You gaze at them as they wheel in endless array before your wondering eyes. Great galaxies stretch before you. Clusters of stars adorn the blackness of the night sky. Across the heavens the band known as the Milky Way appears as a vast and smoky trail. Stars, worlds, planets. Molecules. So would the microscopic creature see you!

The stars in the heavens above appear as points of light with incredible spaces between them. Billions, trillions of stars there are, yet compared to the great empty space they seem few indeed. Given a space ship one could move between stars without touching any. Supposing you could close up the spaces between the stars, the molecules, what would you see? That microscopic creature who is viewing you from afar, is he—it—wondering that also? We knew that all those molecules which the creature sees is us. What, then, is the lineal shape of the star formations in the heavens? Each of us is a Universe, a Universe in which planets—molecules—spin around a central sun. Every rock, twig, or drop of water is composed of molecules in constant, unending motion.

We are composed of molecules in motion. That motion generates a form of electricity which, uniting with the electricity delivered by the Overself, gives sentient life. Around the poles of the Earth magnetic storms flare and glow, giving rise to the Aurora Borealis with all its colored lights. Around all planets—and molecules—magnetic radiations interplay and interact with other radiations emanating from nearby worlds and molecules. "No man is a world unto himself!" No world or molecule can exist without other worlds or molecules. Every creature, world or molecule depends upon the existence of other creatures, worlds or molecules that its own existence may continue.

It must also be appreciated that molecule groups are of different densities; they are, in fact, like clusters of stars swinging in space. In some parts of the Universe there are areas populated by very few stars or planets, or worlds—whichever you like to call them—but elsewhere there is a considerable density of planets, as for example, in the Milky Way. In much the same manner rock can represent a very dense constellation or galaxy. Air is much more thinly populated by molecules. Air, in fact, goes through us and actually passes through the capillaries of our lungs and into our blood stream. Beyond air there is space where there are clusters of hydrogen molecules widely dispersed. Space is not emptiness as people used to imagine, but is a collection of wildly oscillating hydrogen molecules and, of course, the stars and planets and worlds formed from the hydrogen molecules.

It is clear that if one has a substantial collection of molecular groups, then it is quite a difficult matter for any other creature to pass through the groups, but a so-called "ghost" which has its molecules widely spaced can easily pass through a brick wall. Think of the brick wall as it is; a collection of molecules something like a cloud of dust in suspension in the air. Improbable though it may seem, there is space between every molecule just as there is space between different stars, and if some other creatures were small enough, or if their molecules were dispersed enough, then they could pass between the molecules of, say, a brick wall without touching any. This enables us to appreciate how a ghost can appear within a closed room, and how it can walk through a seemingly solid wall. Everything is relative, a wall which is solid to you may not be solid to a ghost or to a creature from the astral. But we shall deal with such things later.

Lesson Two

THE HUMAN BODY is, of course, a collection of molecules as we have just seen, and while every minute creature such as a virus would see us as a collection of molecules, we have to regard the human being now as a collection of chemicals as well.

A human being consists of many chemicals. The human body also consists mainly of water. If you think that contradicts anything in the last lesson remember that even water consists of molecules, and it is indeed a fact that if you could teach a virus to speak, it would undoubtedly tell you that it saw water molecules clashing around each other like pebbles on a beach. An even smaller creature would say that the molecules of air remind it of sand on the seashore. But now we are concerned more with the chemistry of the body.

If you go to a shop and buy a battery for your flashlight you get a container with a case and a carbon electrode in the center—a piece of carbon perhaps as thick as a pencil—and a collection of chemicals packed tightly between the outer case and the central carbon rod. The whole affair is quite moist inside; outside, of course, it is dry. You put this battery in your flashlight and when you operate the switch you get a light. Do you know why? Under certain conditions, metals and carbon and chemicals react together chemically in order to produce something which we call electricity. This zinc container with its chemicals and its carbon rod generate electricity, but there is no electricity within the flashlight battery, it is instead merely a collection of chemicals ready to do its work under certain conditions.

Many people have heard that boats and ships of all kinds generate electricity by just being in salt water. For instance, under certain conditions a boat or a ship which is even resting idly in the sea can generate an electric current between adjacent dissimilar metal plates. Unfortunately if a ship has, for instance, a copper bottom connected to iron upper-works, then unless special arrangements were made, electrolysis (the generation of electric current) would eat away the junction between the two dissimilar metals, that is, the iron and the copper. Of course it never actually happens now for it can be prevented by using what one terms a sacrificial anode. A piece of metal such as zinc, aluminum, or magnesium is positive compared to other common metals such as copper or bronze. Bronze, as you will know, is often used for making ships' propellers. Now, if the sacrificial anode is fastened to the ship or boat below the water line somewhere, and is connected to other submerged metal parts, this sacrificial metal will corrode and waste away, and it will prevent the hull of the ship or the propellers from wasting away. As this metal piece corrodes, it can be replaced. That is just an ordinary part of ship maintenance, and all this is mentioned just to give you an idea of how electricity can be, and is, generated in the most unusual ways.

The brain generates electricity of its own. Within the human body there are traces of metals, even metals such as zinc, and of course we must remember that the human body has the carbon molecule as its basis. There is much water in a body, and traces of chemicals such as magnesium, potassium, etc. These combine to form an electric current, a minute one, but one which can be detected, measured, and charted.

A person who is mentally ill can, by the use of a certain instrument, have his brain waves charted. Various electrodes are placed upon his head and little pens get to work on a strip of paper. As the patient thinks of certain things, the pens draw four squiggly lines which can be interpreted to indicate the type of illness from which the patient is suffering. Instruments such as this are in common use in all mental hospitals.

The brain is, of course, a form of receiving station for the messages which are transmitted by the Overself, and the human brain in its turn can transmit messages, such as lessons learned, experiences gained, etc., to the Overself. These messages are conveyed by means of the silver cord, a mass of high velocity molecules which vibrate and rotate at an extremely divergent range of frequencies, and connects the human body and the human Overself.

The body here on Earth is something like a vehicle operating by remote control. The driver is the Overself. You may have seen a child's toy car which is connected to the child by a long flexible cable. The child can press a button and make the car go forward, or make it stop or go back, and by turning a wheel on this flexible cable the car can be steered. The human body may be likened very roughly to that, for the Overself which cannot come down to the Earth to gain experiences sends down this body which is us on Earth. Everything that we experience, everything that we do or think or hear travels upwards to be stored in the memory of the Overself.

Very highly intelligent men who get inspiration often obtain a message directly—consciously—from the overself by way of the silver cord. Leonardo da Vinci was one of those who was most constantly in touch with his Overself, and so he rated as a genius in almost everything that he did. Great artists or great musicians are those in touch with the Overself on perhaps one or two particular lines, and so they come back and compose by inspiration music or paintings which have been more or less dictated to them by the Greater Powers which control us.

This silver cord connects us to our Overself in much the same way as the umbilical cord connects a baby to its mother. The umbilical cord is a very intricate device, a very complex affair indeed, but it is as a piece of string compared to the complexity of the silver cord. This cord is a mass of molecules rotating over an extremely wide range of frequencies, but it is an intangible thing so far as the human body on Earth is concerned. The molecules are too widely dispersed for the average human sight to see it. Many animals can see it because animals see on a different range of frequencies and hear on a different range of frequencies than humans. Dogs, as you know, can be called by a silent dog whistle—silent because a human cannot hear it, but a dog easily can. In the same way, animals can see the silver cord and the aura because both these vibrate on a frequency which is just within the receptivity of an animal's sight. With practice it is quite easily possible for a human to extend the band of receptivity of their sight in much the same way as a weak person, by practice and by exercise, can lift a weight which normally would be far far beyond his or her physical capabilities.

The silver cord is a mass of molecules, a mass of vibrations. One can liken it to the tight beam of radio waves which scientists bounce off the Moon. Scientists trying to measure the distance of the Moon, broadcast a wave form on a very narrow beam to the surface of the Moon. That is much the same as the silver cord between the human body and the human Overself; it is the method whereby the Overself communicates with the body on Earth.

Everything we do is known to the Overself. People strive to become spiritual if they are on the right path. Basically, in striving for spirituality they strive to increase their own rate of vibration on Earth, and by way of the silver cord to increase the rate of vibration of the Overself. The Overself sends down a part of itself into a human body in order that lessons may be learned and experiences gained. Every good deed we do increases our Earth and our astral rate of vibration, but if we do an evil deed to some person that decreases and subtracts from our rate of spiritual vibration. Thus, when we do an ill turn to another we put ourselves at least one step down on the ladder of evolution, and every good deed we do increases our own personal vibration by a like amount. Thus it is so essential to adhere to the old Buddhist formula which exhorts one to "return good for evil and to fear no man, and to fear no man's deed, for in returning good for evil, and giving good at all times, we progress upwards and never downwards."

Everyone knows of a person who is "a low sort of fellow." Some of our metaphysical knowledge leaks over into common usage in much the same way as we say a person is in a black mood, or a blue mood. It is all a matter of vibration, all a matter of what the body transmits by way of the silver cord to the Overself, and what the Overself sends back again by way of the silver cord to the body.

Many people cannot understand their inability to consciously contact the Overself. It is quite a difficult matter without long training. Supposing you are in South America and you want to telephone someone in Russia, perhaps in Siberia. First of all, you have to make sure that there is a telephone line available, then you have to take into consideration the difference in time between the two countries. Next, you have to make sure that the person you want to telephone is available and can speak your language, and after all that you have to see if the authorities will permit such a telephone message. It is better at this stage of evolution not to bother too much about trying to contact one's Overself consciously, because no course, no information, will give you in a few written pages what it might take ten years of practice to accomplish. Most people expect too much; they expect that they can read a course and immediately go and do everything that the Masters can do, and the Masters may have studied a lifetime, and many lifetimes before that! Read this course, study it, ponder upon it, and if you will open your mind you may be granted enlightenment. We have known many cases where people (most often women) received certain information and they then could actually see the etheric or the aura or the silver cord. We have many such experiences to fortify us in our statement that you, too, can do this—if you will permit yourself to believe!

Lesson Three

WE HAVE ALREADY seen how the human brain generates electricity through the action of the chemicals, the water, and the metallic ores coursing through it and of which it is comprised. Just as the human brain generates electricity so does the body itself, for the blood is coursing through the veins and arteries of the body also carrying those chemicals, those metallic traces, and the water. The blood is, as you well know, mainly water. The whole body is suffused with electricity. It is not the type of electricity which lights your house or heats the stove with which you cook. Look upon it as of magnetic origin.

If one takes a bar magnet and lays it down on a table, placing upon it a sheet of plain paper, and then sprinkles on the plain paper, above the magnet, a liberal supply of iron filings, one will find that the filings arrange themselves in a special pattern. It is worth making the attempt. Get an ordinary cheap magnet from a hardware store or scientific supplier— they are very, very cheap—or you may be able to borrow one. Put a piece of paper across the top so that the magnet underneath is located at about the center of the paper. From your chemist or scientific supply store you will be able to obtain fine iron filings. Here again, they are very, very cheap. Sprinkle them on the paper as you would sprinkle salt or pepper. Let them fall on the paper from a height of perhaps twelve inches, and you will find that these iron filings arrange themselves in a peculiar pattern which precisely follows the magnetic lines of force coming from the magnet. You will find you have the central bar of the magnet outlined, and then you have curved lines going from each end of the magnet. The best way, the most profitable way, is to try it, for this will help you in your later studies. The magnetic force is the same as the etheric of the human body, the same as the aura of the human body.

Probably everyone knows that a wire which carries an electric current has a magnetic field around it. If the current varies, that is, if it is known as alternating instead of direct, then the field pulsates and fluctuates in accordance with the changes in polarity, that is, it seems to pulse with the alternating current. The human body, which is a source of electricity, has a magnetic field outside it. It has a highly fluctuating field. The etheric, as we call it, fluctuates or vibrates so rapidly that it is difficult to discern the movement. In much the same way, one can have an electric lamp lighted in one's house, and although the current fluctuates fifty or sixty times a second, one cannot perceive this, yet in some country districts, or perhaps aboard ship, the fluctuations are so slow that the eye can detect the flickerings.

If a person goes too close to another one there will often be a sensation of goose-flesh. Many people—most people—

are fully aware of the close proximity of another person. Try it on a friend, stand behind your friend and hold one finger close to the nape of his neck and then touch him lightly. He will often not be able to distinguish between a closeness and a touch. That is because the etheric is also susceptible to touch.

This etheric is the magnetic field which surrounds the human body (figure 3). It is the forerunner of the aura, the nucleus of the aura, as one might say. In some people the etheric covering extends for about an eighth of an inch around every part of the body, even around each individual strand of hair. In other people it may extend for some inches, but not often more than six inches. The etheric can be used to measure the vitality of a person. It changes considerably in intensity with the health. If a person has done a hard day's work, then the etheric will be very close to the skin, but after a good rest it will extend perhaps for inches. It follows the exact contours of the body, it even follows the contours of a mole or a pimple. In connection with the etheric, it might be of interest to state that if one is subjected to a very very high tension of electricity at negligible amperage, then the etheric can be seen glowing, sometimes pink, sometimes blue. There is a weather condition also which increases the visibility of the etheric. It is met with at sea and is known as Saint Elmo's Fire. Under certain weather conditions, every part of a ship's masts and rigging become outlined in cold fire, it is quite harmless but rather frightening for those who see it for the first time. One can liken this to the etheric of a ship.

Many people in the country have had the experience of going out into the countryside on a dark or misty night and have looked at the high tension wires stretching overhead. Under suitable conditions they will have noticed a misty whitish-bluish glow, it looks rather eerie, and has given many an honest countryman a severe fright! Electrical engineers know this as the corona of high tension wires and it is one of the

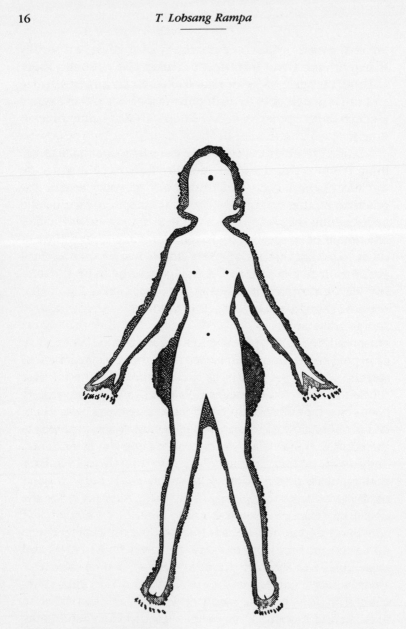

Figure 3. The etheric.

difficulties with which they are confronted, because a corona sweeping down over insulators can ionize the air so that there is a short circuit, and that may trip relays in power stations and put a whole countryside into darkness. In these more modern days, engineers take very special and costly precautions in order to minimize or eliminate the corona. The corona of a human body, of course, is the etheric, and it looks something the same as the discharge from high tension wires.

Most people can see the etheric of the body if they will practice a little, if they will have patience. Unfortunately, people think that there is some quick and cheap way to the attainment of knowledge and powers which take the Masters years. Nothing can be done without practice; great musicians practice for hours every day, they never cease to practice. So you, if you want to be able to see the etheric and the aura, you must practice also. One way is to get a willing subject and get that person to extend a bare arm. Have the fingers outspread, the arm and fingers should be a few inches away from some neutral or black background. Look toward the arm and the fingers, not directly at it, but toward it. There is just a little knack in looking at the right place in the right way. As you look, you will see clinging closely to the flesh something that looks like a bluish-grayish smoke. As we said, it extends perhaps an eighth of an inch, perhaps six inches from the body. Quite often a person will look toward the arm and see nothing but the arm; that may be because they are trying too hard, it may be because they "cannot see the wood for the trees." Let yourself become relaxed, do not try too hard, and with practice you will see that there really is something there.

Another way is to practice on yourself. Sit down and make yourself quite comfortable. Place yourself so that you are at least six feet from any other object, be it chair, table, or wall. Breathe steadily, deeply, and slowly, extend your arms to full length, place your finger tips together with your thumbs upwards so that just your finger tips are in contact. Then, if you part your fingers so that they are about an eighth of an inch—quarter of an inch—apart you will perceive something. It may look like a gray mist, it may look as if it is almost luminous, but when you see that, then very very slowly draw your fingers further apart, a quarter of an inch at a time, you will soon see that there is something there. That something is the etheric. If you should lose contact, that is, if the faint something should vanish, then touch your finger tips together and start all over again. It is just a matter of practice. Once again, the great musicians of this world practice, and practice, and practice; they produce good music after their practice; you can produce good results in metaphysical sciences!

But look again at your fingers. Watch carefully the faint mist flowing from one to the other. With practice you will observe that it flows from either the left hand to the right hand, or from the right hand to the left hand, depending not merely upon your sex, but upon your state of health and what you are thinking at the time.

If you can get an interested person to help you, then you can practice with the palm of your hand. You should get this person, if possible a member of the opposite sex, to sit in a chair facing you. You should both extend your hands, your arms, at full length. Then slowly bring your hand, palm down, close to that of your friend who sits palm up. When you are about two inches apart you may find either a cool breeze or a warm breeze flowing from one hand to the other, the sensation starts in the middle of the palm. It depends on which hand it is and which sex you are whether you feel a cold or a warm breeze. If you feel a warm breeze, move your hand slightly so that your hand is not directly in line fingers to fingers, but at an angle, and you may find that the sensation of heat increases. The heat increases as you practice. When you get to this stage, if you look carefully between your palm and that of the other person, you will see very distinctly the etheric. It is like cigarette smoke which has not been inhaled, that is, instead of the dirty gray of inhaled cigarette smoke it will have a fresh bluish tinge.

We have to keep on repeating that the etheric is merely the outer manifestation of the magnetic forces of the body. We call it the "ghost" because when a person dies in good health this etheric charge remains for a time, it may become detached from the body and wander like a mindless ghost, which is a thing completely and utterly different from the astral entity. We shall deal with all that at a later date. But you may have heard of old graveyards in the country, where there are no street lamps, etc.; many people say that they can see a faint bluish light on dark nights rising up from the ground of a grave which has only that day been made. That is actually the etheric charge dissipating away from a newly dead body. You can say that it is similar to the heat departing from a kettle which has been boiling and has then been switched off. As the kettle gets cooler the feeling of heat from the outer side obviously becomes less. In the same way, as a body dies (there are relative stages of death, remember!) the etheric force gets lower and lower. You can have an etheric hanging around a body for several days after clinical life has departed, but that will form the subject of a separate lesson.

Practice, and practice, and practice. Look at your hands, look at your body, try these experiments with a willing friend, because only by practice can you see the etheric, and until you can see the etheric then you cannot see the aura which is a much finer thing.

Lesson Four

AS WE SAW in the preceding lesson, the body is surrounded by the etheric which encompasses every part of that body. Extending outside the etheric is the aura. This is in some ways similar to the etheric in that it is of magnetic electric origin, but there the similarity ends.

One can state that the aura shows the colors of the Overself. It shows whether a person is spiritual or carnal. It shows also if a person is of good health, or poor health, or is actually diseased. Everything is reflected in the aura, it is the indicator of the Overself, or, if you prefer, of the soul. The Overself and the soul, of course, are the same thing.

In this aura we can see sickness and health, dejection and Success, love and hatred. It is perhaps fortunate that not so many people can see the auras at the present time, for nowadays it seems to be the common thing to take advantage of one, to seek the upper hand, and the aura betrays every thought as it should do, reflecting as it does the colors and the vibrations of the Overself. It is a fact that when a person is desperately ill the aura begins to fade, and in certain cases, the aura actually fades out before a person dies. If a person has had a long illness, then the aura does actually fade out before death, leaving only the etheric. On the other hand, a person who is killed accidentally while in good health possesses the aura up to, and for some moments after, clinical death.

It might be well here to interpose certain remarks about death, because death is not like switching off a current or emptying a bucket. Death is a rather long drawn-out affair. No matter how a person dies, no matter if a person is beheaded even, death does not take place for some moments after. The brain, as we have seen, is a storage cell generating electric current. The blood supplies the chemicals, the moisture and the metallic ores, and inevitably these ingredients become stored in the tissue of the brain. Thus the brain can continue to function for from three to five minutes after clinical death. It is said by some people that this or that form of execution is instantaneous, but that, of course is ridiculous. As we have stated, even if the head is completely severed from the body, the brain can still function for from three to five minutes. There is a case which was actually witnessed and carefully chronicled in the days of the French Revolution. A so-called traitor had been beheaded and the executioner reached down and lifted up the head by the hair, saying as he did so, "This is the head of a traitor." People in the audience—executions in those days were public and also a public holiday—were alarmed when the lips formed the soundless words, "That is a lie." That can actually be seen in the records of the French Government. Any doctor or surgeon will tell you that if the blood supply be interrupted, the brain becomes impaired after three minutes; that is why, if a heart stops, there are such frantic efforts to start the flow of blood again. We have digressed here to show that death is not instantaneous, nor is the fading of the aura. It is medical fact, by the way, known to coroners and pathologists that the body dies at various rates; the brain dies, and then organs die one by one. About the last to die are the hair and nails.

As the body does not die instantly, traces of the aura may linger on. Thus it is that a person who is clairvoyant can see in the aura of a dead person why that person expired. The etheric is of a different nature from the aura, and the etheric may continue for some time as a detached phantom, especially if a person has died violently, suddenly. A person in good health who meets a violent end has his "batteries fully charged," and so the etheric is at full strength. With the death of the body the etheric becomes detached and floats away. By magnetic attraction it will undoubtedly visit its former haunts, and if a clairvoyant person is about or a person who is highly excited (i.e., has his vibrations increased), then that person will be able to see the etheric and will exclaim "Oh! The ghost of so-and-so!"

The aura is of much finer material than the comparatively crude etheric. The aura, in fact, is as much finer to the etheric as the etheric is to the physical body. The etheric flows over the body like a complete covering following the contours of the body, but the aura extends to form an egg-shaped shell around the body (figure 4). It might be, for instance, seven feet or more in height, and about four feet in width at its broadest part. It tapers down so that the narrow end of the egg is at the bottom, that is, where the feet are. The aura consists of the radiations of brilliant color from the various centers of the body to other centers of the body. The old Chinese used to say that, "One picture is worth a thousand words." So, to save a few thousand words, we will insert here in this lesson a sketch of a person standing full face, and side view, and on these sketches we will indicate the lines of force

Figure 4. Main lines of the aura.

of the aura to and from the various centers, and the general
outline of the egg-shape.

We must make it clear also that the aura really does
exist even if you cannot see it for the moment. As you will
appreciate, you cannot see the air which you breathe, and we
doubt if a fish can see the water in which it swims. The aura,
then, is a real, vital force. It exists even though most untrained
people cannot see it. It is possible to see an aura by using
various equipment, there are, for example, various types of
goggles which can be used over the eyes, but all the informa-

tion which we have been able to gather on the subject indicates that these goggles are extremely injurious to the sight; they try the eyes, they force the eyes to act in an unnatural manner, and we cannot recommend for one moment goggles purporting to enable one to see the aura, nor those various screens consisting of two sheets of glass with a watertight space between which one fills with a special and usually highly expensive dye. We can only suggest that you practice and practice, and then with a little faith and a little help you should be able to see. The biggest difficulty in seeing the aura is that most people do not believe that they can see it.

The aura, as we have stated, is of various colors, but we would point out that what we refer to as colors is merely a special part of the spectrum. In other words, although we use the word color we could just as well quote the frequency of that wave which we call red or blue. Red, by the way, is one of the easiest colors to see. Blue is not so easy. There are some people who cannot see blue, there are others who cannot see red. If you are in the presence of a person who can see the aura, by the way, be careful not to say something which is untrue, because if you do tell an untruth the aura-seer will betray you. Normally a person has a halo which is either a bluish or a yellowish color. If a lie is told then a greenish-yellow shoots through the halo. It is a difficult color to explain, but once seen the color is never forgotten. So—to tell a lie is to betray oneself immediately by the greenish-yellow flare which shoots through the halo which is at the top of the aura.

One can say that the aura extends basically up to the eyes, and then you get a radiant layer of yellow or blue which is the halo or nimbus. Then, at the very topmost part of the aura, you get a sort of fountain of light which in the East is known as the Flowering Lotus because it does actually look like that. It is an interchange of colors, and to the imaginative it reminds one irresistibly of the opening of the seven-petalled lotus.

The greater one's spirituality, the more saffron-yellow is the nimbus or halo. If a person has dubious thoughts, then that particular portion of the aura turns an unpleasant muddy brown, fringed by this bile-colored yellowish-green which betokens falsehoods.

We are of the belief that more people see auras than seems apparent. We believe that many people see or sense the aura and do not know what they are seeing. It is quite a common thing for people to say that they must have this or that color, they cannot wear such-and-such a color, because instinctively they think that it would clash with the aura. You may have noticed people who wear clothing which is quite utterly impossible according to your own estimation. You may not see the aura, but you—being possibly more perceptive than your unsuitably clad friends—will know that such colors clash completely with their auras. Many people, then, sense, experience, or are aware of the human aura, but because from early childhood they have been taught that it is nonsense to see this, or nonsense to see that, they have hypnotized themselves into believing that they could not possibly see such a thing.

It is also a fact that one can influence one's health by wearing clothing of certain colors. If you wear a color which clashes with your aura, then you will undoubtedly be ill at ease or self-conscious, you may even be indisposed until you take that unsuitable color off. You may find that a particular color in a room irritates you or soothes you. Colors, after all, are merely different names for vibrations. Red is one vibration, green another vibration, and black is yet another. Just as the vibration which we call sound can clash and make disharmony, so can soundless vibrations which we call colors clash and make a spiritual disharmony.

Lesson Five

IN THIS LESSON we are going to learn more about the colors of the aura. For example, every musical note is a combination of harmonic vibrations which depends upon being compatible with its neighbors. Any lack of compatibility causes a sour note, a note which is not pleasant to hear. Musicians strive to produce only notes which please. As in music, so in colors, for colors also are vibrations, although they are on a slightly different part of the "Human perception Spectrum." One can have pure colors, colors which please and uplift one. Or one can have colors which jar, which jangle the nerves. In the human aura there are many many different colors and shades of colors. Some of them are beyond the range of vision of the observer and so, for those colors we have no universally accepted name.

There is, as you know, a silent dog whistle. That is, it resonates on a band of vibrations which human ears cannot hear. At the other end of the scale, a human can hear deeper sounds than can a dog; low sounds are inaudible to dogs. Suppose we move the range of human hearing up—then we should hear as a dog does and would hear the high notes of the dog whistle. So, if we can raise or shift our sight range up we shall be able to see the human aura. Unless we do it carefully, though, we shall then lose the ability to see black or deep purple.

It would be unreasonable to list innumerable colors. Let us deal with only the most common, the strongest, colors. The basic colors change according to the progress of the person in whose aura they are seen. As the person improves in spirituality, so the color improves. If a person is unfortunate enough to slip back on the ladder of progress, then his basic colors may alter completely or change in shade. The basic colors (which we mention below) show the basic person. The innumerable pastel shades indicate the thoughts and intentions as well as the degree of spirituality. The aura swirls and flows like a particularly intricate rainbow. Colors race round the body in increasing spirals, and also pour down from the head to the feet. But these colors are many more than ever appeared in a rainbow; a rainbow is merely refraction from water crystals—simple things—the aura is life itself.

Here are some notes on a very few colors, very few because there is no point in dealing with others until you can see these listed!

Red

In its good form red indicates sound driving force. Good generals and leaders of men have a lot of clear red in their aura. A particularly clear form of red with clear yellow edges indicates a person who is a crusader—one who is always striving to help others. Do not confuse this with the ordinary meddler; his red would be brown. Clear red bands or flashes emanating from the site of an organ indicates that the organ is in very good health. Some of the world leaders have a lot of clear red in their make-up. Unfortunately, in too many instances, it is contaminated with debasing shades.

A bad red, one that is muddy or too dark, indicates a bad or vicious temper. The person is unreliable, quarrelsome, treacherous, a self-seeker at the expense of others. Dull reds invariably show nervous excitation. A person with "bad" red may be physically strong. Unfortunately he will also be strong at wrong-doing. Murderers always have degraded red in their auras. The lighter the red (lighter, not clearer) the more nervous and unstable the person. Such a person is very active—jittery even—and cannot keep still for more than a few seconds at a time. Of course such a person is very self-centered indeed. Reds around the organs indicate their state. A dull red, brownish red even, slowly pulsing over the site of an organ indicates cancer. One can tell if the cancer is there or if it is incipient. The aura indicates what illnesses are going to afflict the body later, unless curative steps are taken. This is going to be one of the greatest uses of aura therapy in later years.

A speckled, flashing red from the jaws indicates toothache; a dull brown pulsing in time from the nimbus indicates fright at the thought of a visit to a dentist. Scarlet is usually worn by those who are too sure of themselves; it indicates that a person is altogether too fond of himself. It is the color of false pride—pride without a foundation. But—scarlet also shows most clearly around the hips of those ladies who sell love for coins of the realm! They are indeed "Scarlet women!" Such women are usually not at all interested in the sex act as such; to them it is merely a means of earning a living. So, the over-conceited person and the prostitute share the same colors in the aura. It is worth a thought that these old sayings, such as "scarlet woman," "blue mood," "red rage," "black with

temper," and "green with envy," do indeed accurately indicate
the aura of a person afflicted with such a mood. The people
who originated such sayings obviously consciously or unconsciously saw the aura.

Still on with the red group—pink (it is more of a coral,
really) shows immaturity. Teenagers show pink instead of any
other red. In the case of an adult, pink is an indicator of
childishness and insecurity. A red-brown, something like raw
liver, indicates a very nasty person indeed. One who should
be avoided, for he will bring trouble. When seen over an
organ, it shows that the organ is very diseased and the person
who has such a color over a vital organ will soon die.

All people with red showing at the end of the breastbone
(end of the sternum) have nerve trouble. They should learn
to control their activities and live more sedately if they want
to live long and happily.

Orange

Orange is really a branch of red, hut we are paying it the
compliment of giving it a classification of its own because
some religions of the Far East used to regard orange as the
color of the Sun and paid homage to it. That is why there are
so many orange colors in the Far East. On the other hand, just
to show the two sides of the coin, other religions held the
belief that blue was the color of the sun. It does not matter to
which opinion you subscribe, orange is basically a good color,
and people with a suitable shade of orange in their aura are
those who show consideration for other people, they are
humanitarians, people who do their best to help others not
so fortunately endowed. A yellow-orange is to be desired
because it shows self-control, and has many virtues.

Brownish-orange indicates a repressed lazy person who
"couldn't care less." A brownish-orange also indicates kidney

trouble. If it is located over the kidneys and has a jagged gray blur in it, it shows the presence of kidney stones.

An orange which is tinged with green indicates a person who loves to quarrel just for the sake of quarreling, and when you progress to the point when you can see the shades within the shades within the colors, then be wise and avoid arguing with those who have a green amid the orange because they can see "only black and white." They lack imagination, they lack the perception and discernment to realize that there are shades of knowledge, shades of opinion, and shades of color. The person afflicted with a greenish-orange aura argues endlessly just for he sake of argument and without really caring whether the arguments are right or wrong; to such people the argument is the thing.

Yellow

A golden yellow indicates that its possessor is of a very spiritual nature. All the great saints had golden halos around their heads. The greater the spirituality the brighter glowed the golden yellow. To digress, let us state here that those of the very highest spirituality also have indigo, but we are dealing with yellow. Those who have yellow in the aura always are in good spiritual and moral health. They are well upon the path, and according to the exact shade of yellow they have little of which to be afraid.

A person with bright yellow in the aura can be completely trusted. A person with a degraded yellow (the color of bad cheddar cheese) is of a cowardly nature, and that is why people say, "Oh, he is yellow !" It used to be far more common that one could see the aura, and presumably most of these sayings came into the different languages at that time. But a bad yellow shows a bad person, one who is really frightened of everything. A reddish-yellow is not at all favorable because it indicates mental, moral and physical timidity, and with it absolute weakness of spiritual outlook and conviction. People with a reddish-yellow will change from one religion to another, always seeking for something which is not obtainable in five minutes. They lack staying power, they cannot stick at a thing for more than a few moments. A person who has a red-yellow and brown-red in the aura is always chasing after the opposite sex and getting nowhere. It is noteworthy that if a person has red hair (or ginger) and has red-yellow in the aura, that person will be very pugnacious, very offensive, and very ready to misconstrue any remark into a personal slight. This refers particularly to those who have red hair and reddish, perhaps freckled, skin. Some of the redder yellows indicate that the person possessing these shades has a great inferiority complex. The redder the red in the yellow, the greater the degree of inferiority. A brownish-yellow shows very impure thoughts and poor spiritual development. Presumably most people know about Skid Row, the vale to which all drunks, deadbeats, and derelicts eventually drift on this Earth. Many of the people in that class, or condition, have this red-brown-yellow, and if they are particularly bad they have an unpleasant form of lime green speckling the aura. These people can rarely be saved from their own folly.

A brownish-yellow indicates impure thoughts and that the person concerned does not always keep to the straight and narrow path. In the health line a green-yellow shows liver complaints. As the greenish-yellow turns to brownish-reddish-yellow it shows that the complaints are more in the nature of social diseases. A person with a social disease invariably has a dark brown, dark yellow band around the hips. It is often speckled with what looks to be red dust. With the brown becoming more and more pronounced in the yellow, and perhaps showing jagged bands, it indicates mental afflictions. A person who is a dual personality (in the psychiatric sense) will often show one half of the aura as a bluish-yellow and the other half as a brownish or greenish-yellow. It is a thoroughly unpleasant combination.

The pure golden yellow with which we commenced this heading should always be cultivated. It can be attained by keeping one's thoughts and one's intentions pure. Every one of us has to go along through the brighter yellow before we get far along the path of evolution.

Green

Green is the color of healing, the color of teaching, and the color of physical growth. Great doctors and surgeons have a lot of green in their aura; they also have a lot of red, and, curiously enough, the two colors blend most harmoniously and there is no discord between them. Red and green when seen together in materials often clash and offend, but when they are seen in the aura, they please. Green with a suitable red indicates a brilliant surgeon, a most competent man. Green alone without the red indicates a most eminent physician, one who knows his job, or it might indicate a nurse whose vocation is both her career and her love. Green mixed with a suitable blue indicates success at teaching. Some of the greater teachers had green in their auras and bands, or striations, of swirling blue, a form of electric blue. Often between the blue and the green there would be narrow bands of golden yellow which would indicate that the teacher was one who had the welfare of the students at heart and had the necessary high spiritual perceptions in order to teach the best subjects.

All those who are concerned with the health of people and animals have a lot of green in their auric make-up. They may not be high ranking surgeons or physicians, but all people, no matter who they are, if they are dealing with the health of either animals, humans, or plants, all have a certain amount of green in their auras. It seems to be almost their badge of office. Green is not a dominant color, though, it is nearly always subservient to some other color. It is a helpful color and indicates that the person is of a friendly, compassionate, considerate nature. If the person has a yellowish-green aura, however, then that person cannot be trusted, and the more the mixture of unpleasant yellow to unpleasant green, the more untrustworthy, the more unreliable the person. Confidence tricksters (con-men) have a yellow-green—the type of people who talk nicely to people and then swindle them out of their money—these have a sort of lime green to which their yellow is added. As the green turns to blue—usually a pleasant sky blue or electric blue—the more trustworthy a person is.

Blue

This color is often referred to as the color of the spirit world. It also shows intellectual ability as apart from spirituality, but of course it has to be the right shade of blue; with the right shade it is a very favorable color, indeed. The etheric is of a bluish tinge, a blue somewhat similar to non-inhaled cigarette smoke, or the blue of a wood fire. The brighter the blue, the healthier and the more vigorous in health is the person. Pale blue is the color of a person who vacillates a lot, a person who cannot make up his mind, a person who has to be pushed in order to make any worthwhile decision. A darker blue is that of a person who is making progress, a person who is trying. If the blue is darker still it shows one who is keen on the tasks of life and who has found some satisfaction in it. These darker blues are often found in missionaries who are missionaries because they have definitely had "A Call." It is not found in missionaries who just desire a job, perhaps traveling round the world with all expenses paid. One can always judge a person by the vigor of the yellow and the darkness of the blue.

Indigo

We are going to class indigo and violet as being under the same heading because one shades imperceptibly into the other, and it is very much a case of one being quite dependent upon the other. People with indigo showing to a marked extent in their auras are people of deep religious convictions, not merely those who profess to be religious. There is a great deal of difference; some people say that they are religious, some people believe they are religious, but until one can actually see the aura one cannot say for sure; indigo proves it conclusively. If a person has a pinkish tinge in the indigo, the possessor of such a marked aura will be touchy and unpleasant, particularly to those who are under the control of the afflicted person. The pinkish tinge in the indigo is a degrading touch, it robs the aura of its purity. Incidentally, people with indigo, violet, or purple in their auras suffer from heart trouble and stomach disorders. They are the type of people who should have no fried food and very little fat food.

Gray

Gray is a modifier of the colors of the aura. It does not signify anything of itself unless the person is most unevolved. If the person at whom you are looking is unevolved, then there will be great bands and splotches of gray, but you normally would not be looking at the nude body of an unevolved person. Gray in a color shows a weakness of character and a general poorness of health. If a person has gray bands over a particular organ, it shows that the organ is in danger of breaking down, is breaking down, and medical attention should be sought immediately. A person with a dull throbbing headache will have a gray smokey cloud going through the halo or nimbus, and no matter what color the halo, gray bands going through it will pulsate in time with the throb of the headache.

Lesson
Six

BY NOW IT WILL be obvious that everything that is is a vibration. Thus, throughout the whole of existence there is what one could term a gigantic keyboard consisting of all the vibrations which can ever be. Let us imagine that it is the keyboard of an immense piano stretching for limitless miles. (See figure 5 on page 38.) Let us imagine, if you like, that we are ants, and we can see just a very few of the notes. The vibrations will correspond to the different keys of the piano. One note, or key, would cover the vibrations which we term touch, the vibration which is so slow, so solid that we feel it rather than hear it or see it.

The next note will be sound. That is, the note will cover those vibrations which activate the mechanism within our ears. We may not feel those vibrations with our fingers, but

Figure 5. The symbolic keyboard. Readers should note that sight and radio are of an almost identical range of frequencies.

our ears tell us that there is sound. We cannot hear a thing which can be felt, nor can we feel a thing which can be heard. So we have covered two notes on our piano keyboard.

The next will be sight. Here again, we have a vibration of such a frequency (that is, it is vibrating so rapidly) that we cannot feel it and we cannot hear it, but it affects our eyes and we call it sight.

Interpenetrating these three notes there are a very few others such as that frequency, or band of frequencies, which we call radio. A note higher and we get telepathy, clairvoyance, and kindred manifestations or powers. But the whole point is that of the truly immense range of frequencies, or vibrations. We can perceive only a very, very limited range.

Sight and sound are closely related, however. We can have a color and say that it has a musical note because there are certain electronic instruments which have been made which will play a particular note if a color is put under the scanner. If you find that difficult to understand consider this; radio waves, that is, music, speech and even pictures, are around us at all times, they are with us in the house, wherever we go, whatever we do. We—unaided—cannot hear those radio waves, but if we have a special device which we call a radio set which slows down the waves, or, if you like, converts the radio frequencies into audio frequencies, then we can hear the radio program originally broadcast or see the television pictures. In much the same way we can take a sound and say that there is a color to fit it, or we can have a color and say that that particular color has a musical note. This, of course, is well known in the East, and we consider that it does actually increase one's appreciation of art, for example, if one can look at a painting and imagine the chord which would be the result of those colors, if it were made of music.

Everyone will, of course, be aware that Mars is also known as the red planet. Mars is the planet of red, and red of a certain shade—the basic red—has a musical note which corresponds to "do".

Orange, which is a part of red, corresponds to the note "re." Some religious beliefs state that orange is the color of the Sun, while other religions are of the opinion that blue should be the Sun's color. We prefer to state that we hold orange to be the Sun's color.

Yellow corresponds to "me," and the planet Mercury is the ruler of yellow. All this, of course, goes back into ancient Eastern mythology; just as the Greeks had their Gods and Goddesses who raced across the skies in flaming chariots, so the people of the East had their myths and their legends, but they invested the planets with colors, and said that such-and-such a color was ruled by such-and-such a planet.

Green has a musical note corresponding to "fa." It is a color of growth, and it is stated by some people that plants can be stimulated by suitable notes of music. While we have no personal experience on this particular item, we have had information about it from an absolutely reliable source. Saturn is the planet controlling the color green. It may be of interest to state that the ancients derived these colors from the sensations they received as they contemplated a certain planet when they were meditating. Many of the ancients meditated on the highest parts of the Earth, in the high peaks of the Himalayas, for example, and when one is fifteen thousand feet above the surface of the earth, quite a considerable amount of air is left behind, and planets can be seen more clearly, perceptions are more acute. Thus the sages of old laid down the rules about the colors of planets.

Blue has the note of "so." As we mentioned previously, some religions regard blue as the color of the Sun, but we are working in the Eastern tradition and we are going to make the assumption that blue is covered by the planet Jupiter.

Indigo is "la" on the musical scale, and in the East is said to be ruled by Venus. Venus, when favorably aspected, that is, when conferring benefits upon a person, Venus gives artistic ability and purity of thought. It gives the better type of character. It is only when it is connected with lower-vibration people that Venus leads to various excesses. Violet corresponds to the musical note of "ti" and is ruled by the Moon. Here again, if we have a well aspected person, the Moon, or violet, gives clarity of thought, spirituality, and controlled imagination. But if the aspects are poor, then, of course, there are mental disturbances or even lunacy.

Outside the aura there is a sheath which completely encloses the human body, the etheric, and the aura itself. It's as if the whole assembly of the human entity, with the human body at the center, and then the etheric, and then the aura, is all encased in a bag. Imagine it like this; we have an ordinary hen's egg. Inside there is the yolk corresponding to the human body, the physical body, that is. Beyond the yolk we have the white of the egg which we will say represents the etheric and the aura. But then outside the white of the egg, between the white and the shell, there is a very thin skin, quite a tough skin it is, too. When you boil an egg and you get rid of the shell you can peel off this skin; the human assembly is like that. It is all encased in this skin-like covering. This skin is completely transparent and under the impact of swirls or tremors in the aura it undulates somewhat, but it always tries to regain its egg-shape, something similar to a balloon always trying to regain its shape because the pressure within is greater than the pressure without. You will be able to visualize it more if you imagine the body, the etheric, and the aura contained within an exceedingly thin cellophane bag of ovoid shape (see figure 6).

As one thinks, one projects from the brain through the etheric through the aura, and on to the auric skin. Here, upon the outer surface of that covering, one gets pictures of the thoughts. As in so many other instances, this is another example corresponding to radio or television. In the neck of a television tube there is what is known as an electron gun which shoots fast-moving electrons onto a fluorescent screen

Figure 6. Auric sheath.

which is the viewing screen—the part at which you gaze. As the electrons impinge upon a special coating inside the television screen, the thing fluoresces, that is, there is a point of light which persists for a time so that the eyes can carry over by residual memory the picture of where the point of light was. So eventually the human eye sees the whole picture on the television screen. As the picture at the transmitter varies, so does the picture that you see on the television screen vary. In much the same way thoughts go from our transmitter, that is, the brain, and reach that sheath covering the aura. Here the thoughts seem to impinge and form pictures which a clairvoyant can see. But we see not merely the pictures of present thoughts, we can also see what has been.

It is easily possible for an Adept to look at a person and to actually see on the outer covering of the aura some of the things that the subject has done during the past two or three lives. It may sound fantastic to the uninitiated, but nevertheless it is perfectly correct.

Matter cannot be destroyed. Everything that is still exists. If you make a sound, the vibration of that sound—the energy which it causes—goes on forever. If, for instance, you could go from this Earth quite instantly to a far, far planet you would see (provided you had suitable instruments) pictures which happened thousands and thousands of years before. Light has a definite speed, and light does not fade, so that if you got sufficiently distant from the Earth (instantly) you would be able to see the creation of the Earth. But this is taking us away from the subject under discussion. We want to make the point that the subconscious, not being controlled by the conscious, can project pictures of things beyond the present reach of the conscious. And so a person with good powers of clairvoyance can easily see what manner of person faces him. This is an advanced form of psychometry, it is what one might term visual psychometry. We will deal with psychometry later.

Everyone with any perception or sensitivity at all can sense an aura, even when they do not actually see it. How many times have you been instantly attracted, or instantly repelled by a person when you have not even spoken to him? Unconscious perception of the aura explains one's likes and dislikes. All people used to be able to see the aura, but through abuses of various kinds they lost the power. During the next few centuries people are once again going to be able to do telepathy, clairvoyance, etc.

Let us go further into the matter of likes and dislikes: every aura is composed of many colors and many striations of colors. It is necessary that the colors and striations match each other before two people can be compatible. It is often the case that a husband and a wife will be very compatible in one or two directions, and completely incompatible in others. That is because the particular wave form of one aura only touches the wave form of the partner's aura at certain definite points and on those points there is complete agreement and complete compatibility. We say, for instance, that two people are poles apart, and that is definitely the case when they are incompatible. If you prefer, you can take it that people who are compatible have auric colors which blend and harmonize, whereas those who are incompatible have colors which clash and would be really painful to look upon.

People are of certain types. They are of common frequencies. People of a common type go about in a body. You may get a group of young women going about together, or a group of young men lounging on street corners or forming gangs. That is because all these people are of a common frequency or a common type of aura, they depend upon each other, they have a magnetic attraction for each other, and the strongest person in the group will dominate the whole and influence them for good or for bad. Young people should be trained by discipline and by self-discipline to control their more elementary impulses in order that humanity as a whole may be improved.

As already stated, a human is centered within the egg-shape covering—centered within the aura, and that is the normal position for most people—average, healthy people. When people have mental illness they are not properly centered. Many people have said, "I feel out of myself today." That may well be the case, they may be projecting at an angle inside the ovoid. People who are of dual personality are completely different from the average, they may have half the aura of one color, and half of a completely different color pattern. They may—if their dual personality is marked—have an aura which is not just one-egg shape but has two eggs joined together at an angle to each other. Mental illness should not be treated so lightly. Shock treatment can be a very dangerous thing because it can drive the astral (we shall deal with this later) straight out of the body. But in the main shock treatment is designed (consciously or unconsciously) to shock the two eggs into one. Often it just burns out neural patterns in the brain.

We are born with certain potentialities, certain limits as to the coloring of our auras, the frequency of our vibrations and other things, and it is thus possible for determined, well-intentioned people to alter the aura for the better. Sadly, it is much easier to alter it for the worse. Socrates, to take one example, knew that he would be a good murderer, but he was not going to give in to the blows of fate and so he took steps to alter his path through life. Instead of becoming a murderer, Socrates became the wisest man of his age. All of us can, if we want to, raise our thoughts to a higher level and so help our auras. People with brown muddy-colored red in the aura, which shows excessive sexuality, can increase the rate of vibration of the red by sublimating the sexual desires and then they will become people with constructive drives, people who make their way through life.

The aura vanishes soon after death, but the etheric may continue for quite a long time; it depends on the state of health of its former possessor. The etheric can become the mindless ghost which carries out senseless hauntings. Many people in the country districts have seen a form of bluish glow over the graves of those who have just been interred. This glow is particularly noticeable by night. This, of course, is merely the etheric dissipating away from the decomposing body.

In the aura low vibrations give dull muddy colors, colors which nauseate rather than attract. The higher one's vibrations become the purer and the more brilliant become the colors of the aura, brilliant not in a garish way, but in the best, the most spiritual way. One can only say that pure colors are delightful while the muddy colors are distasteful. A good deed brightens one's outlook by brightening one's auric colors. A bad deed makes us feel blue or puts us in a black mood. Good deeds—helping others—make us see the world through "rose colored glasses."

It is necessary to keep constantly in mind that the color is the main indicator of a person's potentialities. Colors change, of course, with one's moods, but the basic colors do not change unless the person improves (or deteriorates) the character. You may take it that the basic colors remain the same, but the transient colors fluctuate and vary according to the mood. When you are looking at the colors of a person's aura you should ask:

1. What is the color?

2. Is it clear or muddy, how plainly can I see through it?

3. Does it swirl over certain areas, or is it located almost permanently over one spot?

4. Is it a continuous band of color holding its shape and its form, or does it fluctuate and have sharp peaks and deep valleys?

We must also make sure that we are not prejudging a person because it is a very simple matter to look at an aura and imagine that we see a muddy color when actually it is not muddy at all. It may be our own wrong thoughts which makes a color appear muddy, for remember, in looking at any other person's aura we first have to look through our own aura.

There is a connection between musical and mental rhythms. The human brain is a mass of vibrations with electrical impulses radiating from every part of it. A human emits a musical note depending upon the rate of vibration of that human. Just as one could get near a beehive and hear the drone of a whole lot of bees, so perhaps could some other creature hear humans. Every human has his or her own basic note which is constantly emitted in much the same way as a telephone wire emits a note in a wind. Further, popular music is such that it is in sympathy with the brain wave formation, it is in sympathy with the harmonic of the body vibration. You may get a hit tune which sets everyone humming and whistling it. People say that they have such-and-such a tune running constantly through their brains. Hit tunes are ones which key into the human brain waves for a certain time before their basic energy is dissipated.

Classical music is of a more permanent nature. It is music which causes our auditory wave form to vibrate pleasantly in sympathy with the classical music. If the leaders of a nation want to rouse up their followers they have to compose, or have composed, a special form of music called a national anthem. One hears the national anthem and one gets filled with all sorts of emotions, then one stands upright and thinks kindly of the country, or thinks fierce thoughts of other countries. That is merely because the vibrations which we call sound have caused our mental vibrations to react in a certain way. Thus it is possible to pre-order certain reactions in a human being by playing certain types of music to that person.

A deep thinking person, one who has high peaks and deep hollows to the brain wave form, likes music of the same type, that is music having high peaks and a deep wave form. But a scatter-brained person prefers the scatter-brain music, music that is more or less a jingle-jangle and on a chart would be represented more or less accurately by just a squiggle.

Many of the greatest musicians are those who consciously or subconsciously can do astral traveling, and who go to the realms beyond death. They hear "the music of the spheres." Being musicians, this heavenly music makes a vast impression upon them, it sticks in their memory so that when they come back to Earth they are immediately in a composing mood. They rush to a musical instrument or to lined paper, and immediately write down, so far as they remember, the notations of the music which they heard in the astral. Then they say—remembering no better—that they have composed this or that work.

The diabolic system of subliminal advertising in which an advertising message is flashed on the television screen too quickly for the conscious eyes to see, plays upon one's semi-awareness while not impinging upon the conscious perceptions. The subconscious is jerked to awareness by the flow of wave patterns reaching it, and the subconscious, being nine-tenths of the whole, eventually drives the consciousness to go out and purchase the item which was advertised even though—consciously—the person concerned knows that he or she does not even desire such a thing. An unscrupulous group of people, such as the leaders of a country who had not the welfare of the people at heart, could actually make the people react to any subliminal commands by using this form of advertising.

Lesson Seven

THIS IS GOING to be a short lesson but a very important one. It is suggested that you read this particular lesson very, very carefully indeed.

Many people, in trying to see the aura, are impatient, they expect to read some written instructions, look up from the printed page, and see auras arrayed before their startled gaze. It is not quite so simple as that. Many of the Great Masters take almost a lifetime before being able to see the aura, but we maintain that provided a person be sincere and will practice conscientiously, the aura can be discerned by the majority of people. It is stated that most people can be hypnotized; in just the same way most people with practice, and that practice really means perseverance, can see the aura.

It must be emphasized over and over again that if one wants to see the aura at its best one has to look upon a nude body, for the aura is influenced considerably by clothing. For example, supposing a person says "Oh! I will put on everything absolutely fresh from the laundry then it will not interfere with my aura!" Well, in all probability some parts of the clothing have been handled by someone at the laundry. Laundry work is monotonous and the people who are engaged upon it normally reflect upon their own affairs. In other words, they are a bit "out of themselves," and as they mechanically fold clothing, or touch the clothing, their thoughts are not upon their work but upon their own private business. The impressions from their own aura enter into the clothing, and then when you go to put on that clothing and look at yourself you are going to find that you have got somebody else's impressions there. Difficult to believe? Look at it this way; you have a magnet and you touch that magnet quite idly with a penknife. Afterwards you find that the penknife has picked up the auric influence of the magnet. It is in much the same way with humans, one can pick up from the other. A woman can go to a show, sit beside a stranger, and afterwards she can say, "Oh, I must have a bath! I feel contaminated being close to that person!"

If you want to see the true aura with all its colors you must look at a nude body. If you can look at a female body you will find that the colors are more distinct. Often with the female body the colors are stronger—more crude if you like— but whatever way you term it, they are still stronger and easier to see. Some of us might find it difficult to go out and discover a woman who will take off her clothes without any objections, so why not use your own body for a change?

You must be alone for this, you must be alone in the privacy of, for example, a bathroom. Make sure that the bathroom has a subdued light. If you find the light is too bright— and it should definitely be dim—hang a towel close to the

Figure 7. "Osglim" type of neon glow lamp.

source of light so that while there is illumination it is of a very
low order. A word of warning here; make sure that the towel
is not so close to the lamp that it smoulders and catches fire;
you are not trying to burn down your house, but to cut down
the light. If you can get hold of one of those Osglim lamps
which use no current that registers on a meter, then you will
find that is very very suitable indeed. An Osglim lamp consists
of a clear glass bulb. From the glass pinch inside the bulb there
is a short rod to which is affixed a round circular plate. Another
rod comes out of the glass pinch and extends almost to the
top of the bulb, and from it hangs a coarse spiral of quite
heavy wire. When this lamp is inserted into a lamp socket and
switched on, it glows with a reddish glow. We are going to
include an illustration of this type of lamp because, of course,
"Osglim" is a trade name, and in different localities the name
may be varied. (See figure 7.)

With the Osglim switched on, or with your illumination
of a definitely dim order, take off all your clothes and look at
yourself in a full-length mirror. Do not try to see anything for
the moment, just relax. Make sure that you have a darkish

curtain behind you, either black (for preference) or dark gray, so that you have what is known as a neutral background, that is, a background which has no color to influence the aura itself.

Wait a few moments while gazing at yourself in the mirror quite idly. Look at your head, can you see a bluish tinge around your temples? Look round your body, from your arms to your hips, for instance. Do you see a bluish flame almost like alcohol flame? You have all seen the type of lamp which some jewelers use which burns methylated spirits or wood alcohol or any of those spirituous liquids. The flame is a bluish flame, often it sparkles yellow at the tips. The etheric flame is like that. When you see that, you are making progress. You may not see it the first, the second, or the third time that you try. In the same way, a musician cannot always get the results that he wants on the first, the second or third time that he plays a difficult piece of music. The musician persevered, so must you. With practice you will be able to see the etheric. With more practice you will be able to see the aura. But again, and again, we must repeat, it is much easier, much clearer with a nude body.

Do not think that there is anything wrong with the nude body. People state "Man is made in the image of God," so what is wrong in seeing "the image of God" unclad? Remember, "To the pure, all things are pure." You are looking at yourself or at another person for a pure reason. If you have impure thoughts you will not see either etheric or aura, you will only see what you are looking for.

Keep looking at yourself, keep looking for this etheric. You will find that in time you can see it.

Sometimes a person will be looking for an aura and see nothing, but instead there will be an itching in the palms, or in the feet, or even in some other part of the body. It is a sensation, this itching, and is absolutely unmistakable. When you get that it means that you are well on the way to seeing, it means that you are stopping yourself from seeing by being too tense; you have to relax, you have to simmer down. If you relax, if you unwind, then instead of getting itching and perhaps twitches you will see the etheric or the aura, or both.

The itching is actually a concentration of your own auric force within your palms (or whatever the center may be). Many people, when they are frightened or tensed up, perspire in the palms of the hands or in the armpits or elsewhere. In this psychic experiment, instead of perspiring, you itch. It is, we repeat, a good sign. It means—we repeat this also—that you are trying too hard and when you are ready to relax, then the etheric and perhaps the aura also will be before your quite startled gaze.

Many people cannot see their own aura with complete accuracy because they are looking through their aura out toward a mirror. The mirror distorts the colors somewhat and reflects back (again through the aura) this distorted range of colors, and so the poor percipient imagines that he or she had muddier colors than may be the case. Think of a fish deep in a pond, looking up at some flower held a few feet from the surface of the water. The fish would not perceive colors the same as you would, the fish would have the vision of the flower distorted by ripples on the water and by the clarity or otherwise of the water. In the same way, you looking out of the depths of your own aura, and seeing the reflected image back into the depths of your own aura, could be misled somewhat. For that reason it is better, whenever convenient, to gaze upon someone else.

Your subject must be quite willing, quite cooperative. If you are looking upon the nude form of some person, often the person gazed upon will be nervous or embarrassed. In that case the etheric shrinks back almost into the body, and the aura itself closes up quite a lot and falsifies the colors. It needs practice to be able to give a good diagnosis, but the main thing is to see any colors first, it doesn't matter if they are true or false colors.

The best way is to get this person and talk to her, just make small talk, just make idle discussion in order to set her at ease and show that nothing is going to happen. As soon as your subject relaxes her etheric will regain its normal proportions and the aura itself will flow out to completely fill the auric sac.

This can in many ways be likened to hypnotism; a hypnotist doesn't just grab a person and hypnotize him then and there on the spot. Usually there are a number of sessions; the hypnotist first sees the patient and they establish a form of rapport, or common basis—a mutual understanding, if you like—and the hypnotist may even try one or two little tricks, such as seeing if the subject responds to elementary hypnotism. After two or three sessions, the hypnotist puts the subject thoroughly into a trance. In much the same way you would have your subject, and first of all do not stare at the body, hardly look at the body, just be natural, as if the other person was fully clothed. Then, perhaps on the second occasion, the subject will be more reassured, more confident, more relaxed. On the third occasion you can indeed look at the body, or look at the outline of the body and see—can you see that faint blue haze? Can you see those bands of colors swirling about the body, and that yellow halo? Can you see that play of light from the top center of the head splaying out like an unfolding lotus, or—in Western parlance—something like a firework sparkler sparkling in various colors?

This is a short lesson; it is an important lesson. Now it is suggested that you wait until you are comfortable, no particular worries on your mind, you are not hungry nor are you overfed, then go to your bathroom, have a bath if you like to get rid of any influence from your clothing, and then practice so that you can see your own aura.

It is all a matter of practice!

Lesson Eight

IN PREVIOUS LESSONS we have regarded the body as being the center of the etheric and the aura; we have moved from the body outward, discussing the etheric and then on to a description of the aura with its striations of color, and forward to the outer auric skin. All this is extremely important, and you are advised to go back and reread the previous lessons, for in this lesson and lesson nine we are going to prepare the ground for leaving the body. Unless you are clear about etheric and aura and the nature of the molecular structure of the body you may run into some difficulties.

The human body consists, as we have seen, of a mass of protoplasm. It is a mass of molecules spread out over a certain volume of space in much the same way as a universe occupies a certain volume of space. Now we are going to go inward, away from the aura, away from the etheric, and into the body, for this flesh-body is just a vehicle, just "a suit of clothes—the garb of an actor who is living out his allotted part upon the stage which is the world."

It has been stated that two objects cannot occupy the same space. That is reasonably correct when one thinks of bricks, or timbers, or pieces of metal, but if two objects have a dissimilar vibration, or if the spaces between their atoms and neutrons and protons are wide enough, then another object can occupy the same space. You may find that difficult to understand so let us put it in a different way, let us give perhaps two illustrations. Here is the first:—

If you get two glasses and you fill them right up to the brim with water you will find that if you tip a little sand—say, a teaspoonful—into one of the filled glasses, the water will overflow and will run down the side, showing that in this case the water and the sand cannot both occupy the same space, and so one has to give way. The sand, being heavier, sinks to the bottom of the glass, thus raising the level in the glass to the point where the water overflows.

Let us turn to the other glass which also has been filled with water to the brim—filled to precisely the same level as the first glass. If now we take sugar and we slowly sprinkle sugar into the glass, we find that we may be able to put even six teaspoonfuls of sugar into the glass before the water overflows. If we do this slowly we will see the sugar disappear, in other words, it dissolves. As it dissolves, its own molecules occupy spaces between water molecules, and thus it does not take up any more space. Only when all the space between the water molecules has been filled with sugar molecules does the excess sugar pile up on the bottom of the glass and eventually cause the water to overflow. In this case we have clear proof that two objects can occupy the same space.

Let us have another illustration; let us look at the solar system. This is an object, an entity, a "something." There are molecules, or atoms which we call worlds, moving about in space. If it is true that two objects cannot occupy the same space, then we could not send a rocket from the Earth into space. Nor could people from another universe enter this universe because if they did so they would be occupying our space. So—under suitable conditions—it is possible for two objects to occupy the same space.

The human body, consisting of molecules with a certain amount of space between atoms, also houses other bodies, tenuous bodies, spirit bodies, or what we call astral bodies. These tenuous bodies are precisely the same as to composition as is the human body, that is, they consist of molecules. But just as earth or lead or wood consists of a certain arrangement of molecules—molecules of a certain density—spirit bodies have their molecules fewer and farther between each. Thus it is quite possible for a spirit body to fit into a flesh body in the most intimate contact, and neither occupies space needed by the other.

The astral body and the physical body are connected together by the silver cord. This latter is a mass of molecules vibrating at a tremendous speed. It is in some ways similar to the umbilical cord which connects a mother to her baby; in the mother impulses, impressions, and nourishment flow from her to the unborn baby. When the baby is born and the umbilical cord is severed, then the baby dies to the life it knew before, that is, it becomes a separate entity, a separate life, it is no longer a part of the mother, so it dies as part of the mother and takes on its own existence.

The silver cord connects the Overself and the human body, and impressions flash from one to the other during every minute of the flesh-body's existence. Impressions, commands, lessons, and at times even spiritual nourishment come down from the Overself to the human body. When death takes place the silver cord is severed and the human body is left like a discarded suit of clothes while the spirit moves on.

This is not the place to go into the matter, but it should be stated that there are a number of spirit bodies. We are dealing with the flesh-body and the astral body at present. In all in our present form of evolution there are nine separate bodies, each connected to the other by a silver cord, but we are concerned now more with astral traveling and matters intimately connected with the astral plane.

A human being, then, is a spirit briefly encased in a body of flesh and bones, encased in order that lessons may be learned and experiences undergone, experiences which could not be obtained by the spirit without the use of a body. Our flesh-body is a vehicle which is driven, or manipulated by the Overself. Some prefer to use the term soul, we use Overself because it is more convenient, the soul is a different matter, actually, and goes to an even higher realm. The Overself is the controller, the driver of the body. The brain of the human is a relay station, a telephone exchange, a completely automated factory, if you like. It takes messages from the Overself, and converts the Overself's commands into chemical activity or physical activity which keeps the vehicle alive, causes muscles to work, and causes certain mental processes. It also relays back to the Overself messages and impressions of experiences gained.

By escaping from the limitations of the body, like a driver temporarily leaving an automobile, we can see the greater world of the spirit and can assess the lessons learned while encased in the flesh, but here we are discussing the physical and the astral with, perhaps, brief mentions of the Overself. We mention the astral in particular because while in that body we can travel to distant places in the twinkling of an eye, we can go anywhere at any time, and can even see what old friends or relations are doing. With practice, we can visit the cities of the world and the great libraries of the world. It is easy, with practice, to visit any library and to look at any book or any page of a book. Most people think they cannot leave the body because in the Western world they have been so conditioned for the whole of their lives to disbelieve in things which cannot be felt, torn to pieces and then discussed in terms which mean nothing.

Children believe in fairies; there are such things, of course, only we who can see them and converse with them call them Nature Spirits. Many really young children have what are known as invisible playmates. To adults, the children live in a world of make-believe, talking animatedly to friends who cannot be seen by the cynical adult. The child knows that these friends are real.

As the child grows older, parents laugh, or become angry at the idle imaginations. Parents, who have forgotten their own childhood and forgotten how their parents acted, get angry with their child for being a liar, or being over-imaginative. Eventually, the child becomes hypnotized into believing that there are no such things as Nature Spirits (or fairies), and in turn these children grow up, have families of their own, and discourage their own children from seeing or playing with Nature Spirits.

We are going to say quite definitely that the people of the East and the people of Ireland know better; there are Nature Spirits, never mind if they are called fairies or leprechauns—never mind whatever they are called—they are real, they do good work, and we, in our ignorance and boastfulness in denying the existence of these people, deny ourselves a wondrous treat and a marvelous store of information, for the Nature Spirits help those whom they like, help those who believe in them.

There are no limits to the knowledge of the Overself. There are very real limits to the abilities of the body—the physical body. Almost everyone on Earth leaves the body during sleep. When they awake they say that they have had a dream, because, here again, humans are taught to believe that this life on Earth is the only one that matters, they are taught that they do not go traveling around when asleep. So, wonderful experiences are rationalized into dreams.

Many people who believe can leave the body at will, and can travel far and fast, returning to the body hours later with a full and complete knowledge of all they have done, all they have seen, and all they have experienced. Nearly anyone can leave the body and do astral traveling, but they have to believe that they can do this, it is quite useless for a person to put out repelling thoughts of disbelief, or thoughts that they cannot do such a thing. Actually, it is remarkably easy to astral travel when one gets over the first hurdle of fear.

Fear is the great brake. Most people have to suppress the instinctive fear that to leave the body is to die. Some people are deathly afraid that if they leave the body they may not be able to get back, or that some other entity will enter the body. This is quite impossible unless one opens the gate by fear. A person who does not fear can have no harm whatever occur. The silver cord cannot be broken when one is astral traveling, no one can invade the body unless one gives a definite invitation by being terrified.

You can always return to your body, just the same as you always awaken after a night of sleep. The only thing to be afraid of is of being afraid; fear is the only thing which causes any danger. We all know that the things which we fear rarely happen.

Thought is the main drawback after fear, because thought, or reason, poses a real problem. These two, thought and reason, can stop one from climbing high mountains; reason tells us that a slip will cause us to be cast down and dashed to pieces. So thought and reason should be suppressed. Unfortunately they have bad names. Thought! Have you ever thought about thought? What is thought? Where do you think? Are you thinking from the top of your head? Or from the back of your head? Are you thinking in your eyebrows? Or in your ears? Do you stop thinking when you close your eyes? No! Your thought is wherever you concentrate; you think wherever you concentrate upon. This simple, elementary fact can help you get out of your body and into the astral, it can help your astral body soar as free as the breeze. Think about it, reread this lesson so far, and think about thought, think how thought has often kept you back because you thought of obstacles, you thought of unnamed fears. You may, for instance, have been alone in the house at midnight with the wind howling outside, and you may have thought of burglars, you may have imagined someone hiding behind a curtain ready to jump upon you. Thought, here, can harm! Think of thought some more.

You are suffering from a toothache, and reluctantly you go to see the dentist. He tells you that you have to have a tooth extracted, you are afraid it will hurt; you sit there in the dental chair in fear. As soon as the dentist picks up his hypodermic to give you an injection, you automatically wince, and perhaps even turn pale. You are sure it is going to hurt, you are sure that you are going to feel that needle going in, and afterward there will be that horrid wrench as your tooth comes bloodily out. Perhaps you are afraid that you are going to faint with the shock, so you feed the fear, you make your tooth hurt more and more by thinking and concentrating the whole of your thought power upon the site of that tooth. All your energy is devoted to making that tooth ache more, but when you idly think, where is the thought then? In the head? How do you know? Can you feel it there? Thought is where you concentrate, thought is within you only because you are thinking of yourself and because you think thought must be within you. Thought is where you want it to be, thought is where you direct it to be.

Let us look at "thought is where you concentrate" again. In the heat of battle, men have been shot or stabbed and have felt no pain. For a time they may not even have known that they were wounded, only when they had time to think about it did they feel the pain and perhaps collapse with shock. But thought, reason, fear, are the brakes that slow up our spiritual evolution, they are but the weary clanking of the machine slowing down and distorting the commands of the Overself.

When we are uncluttered by our own stupid fears and restrictions, we could almost be superhuman, with greatly enhanced powers, both muscular and mental. Here is an example; a weakly, timid man with perfectly shocking muscular development, steps off a sidewalk into a heavy stream of traffic. His thoughts are far, far away, perhaps on his business or upon what sort of a mood his wife is going to be in when he gets home that night. He may even be thinking of unpaid bills. A sudden hoot from an approaching car and the man—without thought—springs back into the sidewalk with a prodigious leap which would normally be quite impossible for even a trained athlete. If this man had been hampered by thought processes he would have been too late, the car would have knocked him over. The lack of thought enabled the ever-watching Overself to galvanize the muscles with a shot of chemicals (such as adrenalin) which made the subject leap far beyond his normal capability and indulge in a spurt of activity beyond the speed of conscious thought.

Humanity in the Western world has been taught that thought, reason, distinguishes us from the animals. Uncontrolled thought keeps us lower than many animals in astral travel. Almost anyone would agree that cats, to give just one example, can see things that humans cannot. Most people have had some experience of animals looking at a ghost or becoming aware of incidents long before the human became so aware. Animals use a different system from reason and thought. So can we!

First, though, we have to control our thoughts, we have to control all those weary tag ends of idle thought which constantly creep past our minds. Sit down somewhere where you are comfortable, where you can be completely relaxed, and where no one can disturb you. If you wish, extinguish the light, for light is a drawback in a case such as this. Sit idly for a few moments just thinking about your thoughts, look at your thoughts, see how they keep creeping into your consciousness, each one clamoring for attention, that quarrel with someone at the office, the unpaid bills, the cost of living, the world situation, what you would like to say to your employer— sweep them all aside!

Imagine that you are sitting on a completely dark roof at the top of a skyscraper; before you there is a large picture window covered by a black blind, a blind which has no pattern, nothing which could prove a distraction. Concentrate on that blind. First of all make sure that there are no thoughts crossing your consciousness (which is that black blind), and if thoughts do tend to intrude, push them back over the edge. You can do so, it is merely a matter of practice. For some moments thoughts will try to flicker at the edge of that black blind, push them back, forcibly will them to go, then concentrate on the blind again, will yourself to lift it so that you may look out at all that is beyond.

Again, as you gaze at that imaginary black blind you will find that all manner of strange thoughts tend to intrude, they try to force their way into the focus of your attention. Push them back, push them back with a conscious effort, refuse to allow those thoughts to intrude (yes, we are aware that we have said this before, but we are trying to drive the point home). When you can hold an impression of complete blankness for a short time, you will find that there is a snap as if a piece of parchment is being torn, then you will be able to see away from this ordinary world of ours, and into a world of a different dimension where time and distance have an entirely fresh meaning. By practicing this, by doing this, you will find that you are able to control your thoughts as do the Adepts and the Masters.

Try it, practice it, for if you want to be able to progress you must practice and practice until you can overcome idle thoughts.

Lesson Nine

IN THE LAST LESSON we dealt in the concluding stages with thought. We said "thought is where you want it to be." That is a formula which really can assist us to get out of the body, to do astral traveling. Let us repeat it.

Thought is where you want it to be. Outside of you, if you want it so. Let us have a little practice. Here again, you will need to be where you are quite alone, where there are no distractions. You are going to try to get yourself out of your body. You must be alone, you must be relaxed, and we suggest that for ease you lie down, preferably upon a bed. Make sure that no one can intrude and ruin your experiment. When you are settled, breathing slowly, thinking of this experiment, concentrate on a point six feet in front of you, close your eyes, concentrate, will yourself to think that you, the real you, the astral you, watches your body from some six feet away. Think! Practice! Make yourself concentrate. Then, with practice, you will suddenly experience a slight, almost electric shock, and you will see your body lying with eyes closed some six feet away.

At first it will be quite an effort to achieve this result. You may feel as if you are inside a big rubber balloon, pushing, pushing. You push and push and strain, and nothing seems to happen. It almost seems to happen. Then at last, suddenly, you burst through, and there is a slight snapping sensation almost as, in fact, puncturing a child's toy balloon. Do not be alarmed, do not give way to fright, because if you remain free from fright you will go on and on, and not have any trouble whatever in the future, but if you are afraid you will bounce back into the physical body and will then have to start all over again at some other date. If you bounce back into your body there is no point in trying anything more that day, for you will rarely succeed. You will need sleep—rest—first.

Let us go further, let us imagine that you have got out of your body with this simple easy method, let us imagine that you are standing there looking at your physical component and wondering what to do next. Do not bother to look at your physical body for the moment, you will see it again quite often! Instead try this:—Let yourself float about the room like a lazily drifting soap bubble, for you do not even weigh as much as a soap bubble now. You cannot fall, you cannot hurt yourself. Let your physical body rest at ease. You will, of course, have dealt with that before freeing your astral from this fleshly sheath. You will have made sure that your flesh body was quite at ease. Unless you took this precaution you may find when you return to it that you have a stiff arm or a cricked neck. Be certain that there are no rough edges that would press into a nerve, for if, for example, you have left your physical body so that an arm is extended over the edge of the mattress there may be some pressure upon a nerve which will cause you "pins and needles" later. Once again, then, make sure that your body is absolutely at ease before making any attempt to leave it for the astral body.

Now let yourself drift, let yourself float about the room, idly move round as if you were a soap bubble drifting on vagrant currents. Explore the ceiling and the places where you could not normally see. Become accustomed to this elementary astral travel because until you are accustomed to idling about in a room you cannot safely venture outside.

Let us try it again with somewhat different wording. Actually, this astral travel affair is easy, there is nothing to it so long as you allow yourself to believe that you can do it. Under no circumstances, under no conditions should you feel fear, for this is not a place for fear, in astral travel you are journeying to freedom. It is only when back in the body that you need to feel imprisoned, encased in clay, weighted down by a heavy body which does not respond very well to spiritual commands. No, there is no place for fear in astral travel, fear is quite alien to it.

We are going to repeat astral travel directions under slightly different wording. You are lying flat on your back on a bed. You have made sure that every part of you is comfortable, there are no projections sticking into nerves, your legs are not even crossed, because if they were, at the point where they cross you might have a numbness after, just because you will have interfered with the circulation of the blood. Rest calmly, contentedly, there are no disturbing influences, nor are you worried. Think only of getting your astral body out of your physical body.

Relax and relax yet more. Imagine a ghostly shape corresponding roughly to your physical body, gently disengaging from the flesh body and floating upwards like a puffball on a light summer's breeze. Let it rise up, keep your eyes closed otherwise, for the first two or three times, you may be so startled that you will twitch, and that twitch may be violent enough to "reel in" the astral to its normal place within the body.

People frequently jerk in a peculiar manner just when they are falling asleep. All too often it is so violent that it brings one back to full wakefulness. This jerk is caused by a too rough separation of the astral body and the physical body, for, as we have already stated, nearly everyone does astral traveling by night even if so many people do not consciously remember their journeyings. But back to our astral body again.

Think of your astral body gradually, easily separating from the physical body, and drifting upward to about three, or perhaps four feet above the physical. There it rests above you swaying gently. You may have experienced a sensation of swaying just when you are falling asleep; that was the astral swaying. As we have said, the body is floating above you, possibly swaying a little, and connected to you by the silver cord which goes from your umbilicus to the umbilicus of the astral body (figure 8 on page 70).

Do not look too closely because we have already warned you that if you become startled and twitch, you will bring your body back and have to start all over again on some other occasion. Suppose you heed our warning, and do not twitch, then your astral body will remain floating above for some moments, take no action at all, hardly think, breathe shallowly for this is your first time out, remember, your first time consciously out, and you have to be careful.

If you are not afraid, if you do not twitch, the astral body will slowly float off, it will just drift away to the end or the side of the bed where quite gently, without any shock whatsoever, it will gradually sink so that the feet touch, or almost touch the floor. Then, the process of making a soft landing over, your astral will be able to look at your physical and relay back what it sees.

You will have a quite discomforting sensation of looking at your own physical body and we point out now that it is often a humiliating experience. Many of us have a completely erroneous idea of what we look like. Do you remember when you first heard your voice? Have you heard your voice on a tape recorder? For the first time you may have frankly disbelieved that it was your voice, you may have thought that someone was playing a trick on you, or that the recorder was faulty.

The first time you hear your voice, you disbelieve it, you become appalled and mortified. But wait until you see your body for the first time. You will stand there in your astral body with your consciousness quite fully transferred to your astral body, and you will look down upon that reclining physical body. You will be horrified; you will not like the shape of the body nor the complexion, you will be shocked at the lines on the face and by the features, and if you advance a little further and look into your mind you will see certain little quirks and phobias which may even cause you to jump back into the body out of sheer fright! But supposing you surmount this first frightening meeting with yourself, what then? You must decide where you are going, what you want to do, what you want to see. The easiest system is to visit some person with whom you are well acquainted, perhaps a close relative who lives in a neighboring city. First it should always be a person that you frequently visit because you have to visualize the person in considerable detail, you have to visualize where he or she lives and precisely how to get there. Remember this is new to you—new to you doing it consciously, that is—and you want to follow the exact route which you would follow if you were going in the flesh.

Leave your room, move to the street (in the astral, of course, but do not worry, people cannot see you), traverse the path which you would normally take keeping fixed before

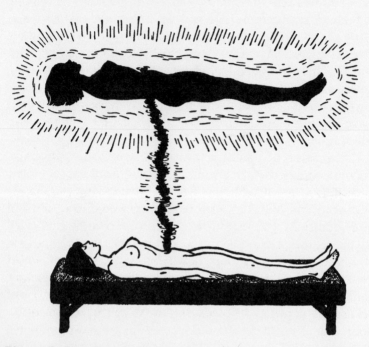

Figure 8. Leaving the body.

you the image of the person whom you want to visit and how to get there. Then, very very speedily, far more quickly than the fastest car could take you, you will be at your friend's or relative's house.

With practice you will be able to go anywhere, seas, oceans and mountains will be no bar, no obstacle, to your path. The lands of the world and the cities of the world will be yours to visit.

Some people think "Oh! Supposing I go and I cannot get back. What then?" The answer is—you cannot get lost. It is quite impossible to get lost, it is quite impossible to harm yourself or to find that your body has been taken over. If anyone comes near to your body while you are astral traveling, the body relays a warning and you are reeled in with the speed of thought. No harm can come to you, the only harm is fear. So do not fear, but experiment, and with experiment will come a realization of all your hopes, all your ambition in the realms of astral travel.

When you are in the astral stage consciously you will see colors more brilliantly than you do in the flesh. Everything will shimmer with life, you may even see particles of life about you like specks. That is the vitality of the earth, and as you pass through it you will pick up strength and courage.

A difficulty is this; you cannot take anything with you, you cannot bring anything back! It is, of course, possible under some conditions—and this comes with much practice only—that you materialize in front of a clairvoyant, but it is not easy to go to a person and carry out a diagnosis of their health condition because you really need to be able to discuss things like that. You can go to a shop and look over their stock and decide what you want to go and buy the next day, that is quite permissible. Often when you visit a shop in the astral you will see the flaws and the shoddiness of some of the goods which are high priced. When you are in the astral and you want to return to the physical, you should keep calm, you should let yourself think of the flesh-body, think that you are going to go back and that you are going to get in. As you think this, there will be a blur of speed or there may even be an instantaneous shift from wherever you were to a spot three or four feet above your reclining body. You will find that you are there, drifting, undulating slightly, just as when you left the body. Let yourself sink down very, very slowly, it must be slowly because the two bodies have to be absolutely synchronized.

If you do it right you will sink into the body without a jar, without any tremor, without any sensation other than that the body is a cold and heavy mass.

If you should be clumsy and you should not exactly align your two bodies, or if someone should interrupt you so that you go back with a jerk, you may find that you have a headache, an almost migraine type of headache. In that case, you have to try to get yourself to sleep, or force yourself out into the astral again, because until your two bodies are back in exact alignment you cannot get rid of the headache. It is nothing to worry about because a quite definite cure is to go to sleep, even for a few moments, or consciously to get out into the astral again.

You may find that back in your flesh-body you are stiff. You may find that the sensation is much the same as putting on a suit of clothes which got wet the day before and now is still wet and dank. Until you get used to it, it is not altogether a happy sensation coming back to the body, you will find that the glorious colors which you saw in the astral world have dimmed. Many of the colors you will not see at all in the flesh, many of the sounds that you heard in the astral are quite inaudible when in the fleshly body. But never mind, you are upon Earth to learn something, and when you have learned that which was your purpose in coming to Earth you will be free of the ties, free of the bonds of Earth, and when you leave your fleshly body permanently, with the silver cord severed, you go to realms far above that of the astral world.

Practice this astral traveling, practice it and practice it. Keep away all fear, for if you have no fear, then there is nothing to fear, no harm can come to you, only pleasure.

Lesson
Ten

WE HAVE SAID "There is nothing to fear except fear." We must emphasize again that provided a person remains free from fear there is no danger whatsoever in astral traveling, no matter how far nor how fast one goes. But, you may ask, what is there to fear? Let us devote this lesson to the subject of fear and what there is that should not be feared! Fear is a very negative attitude, an attitude that corrodes our finer perceptions. No matter of what we are afraid, any form of fear does harm. People may fear that in going into the astral state they may not be able to return to the body. It is always possible to return to the body unless one is actually dying, unless one has come to the end of one's allotted span upon Earth, and that, as you will agree, has nothing to do with astral traveling. It is possible, we must admit, that one can be so afraid as to be paralyzed with fright, and in that case one just cannot do anything. In such a condition a person may be in the astral body and may be so utterly terrified that even the astral body is unable to move. Of course that delays the return to the physical body for some time, until the sharpness of the fear wears off. Fear does wear off, you know, a sensation can be sustained only for a certain time. So a person who is afraid merely delays a perfectly safe return to the physical body.

We are not the only form of life in the astral just as humans are not the only form of life on Earth. In this world of ours we have pleasant creatures like cats and dogs and horses and birds, to mention just a few; but there are also unpleasant creatures like spiders that bite or snakes that poison. There are unpleasant things like germs, microbes and other harmful and noxious things. If you had seen germs under a high powered microscope you would see such fantastic creatures that you would imagine that you were living in the days of the dragons of fairy tale fame.

In the astral world there are many things stranger than anything you can encounter on Earth. In the astral we shall meet remarkable creatures or people or entities. We shall see Nature Spirits; these, by the way, are almost invariably good and pleasant. But there are horrible creatures who must have been seen by some of the writers of mythology and legend, because these creatures are like the devils, the satyrs, and other various aspected fiends of the myths. Some of these creatures are low elementals who may later become human or they may branch out into the animal kingdom. Whatever they may be, at this stage of their development they are thoroughly unpleasant.

It is worth pausing a moment here to point out that drunkards, those who see "pink elephants" and various other remarkable apparitions, are indeed seeing precisely that type of creature. Drunkards are people who have driven their astral body out of the physical body and into the very lowest planes of the astral world. Here they meet truly fearsome creatures, and when the drunkard later recovers—as much as he ever does—his senses, then he has quite a vivid memory of the things that he saw. While getting thoroughly drunk is one method of getting into the astral world and remembering, it is not one which we would recommend because it takes one only to the very lowest, to the most degraded planes of the astral.

There are various drugs now in use by the medical profession (principally in hospitals for the mentally sick) which have a similar effect. Mescaline, for example, can so alter one's vibrations that one is literally ejected from the physical body and catapulted into the astral world. Here again, this is not a method to be recommended. Drugs and other forms of getting out of the physical body are truly harmful, they cause harm to the Overself.

But let us return to our elementals. What do we mean by elementals? Well, elementals are a primary form of spirit life. They are a stage up from thought forms. These thought forms are merely projections from the conscious or unconscious mind of the human and they have merely a pseudo life of their own. Thought forms were created by the ancient Egyptian priests in order that the mummified bodies of great pharaohs and famous queens could be protected from those who would desecrate the ancient tombs. Thought forms are constructed with the idea that they shall repel invaders, that they shall attack by impinging upon the consciousness of those who would intrude, and, in impinging upon the consciousness, to cause such extreme terror that the would be burglar flees. We are not concerned with thought forms, for they are mindless entities which are merely charged by long dead priests and set to accomplish certain tasks, the guarding of tombs against invaders. We are concerned for the moment with elementals.

Elementals, as we have stated, are spirit people in the early stages of development. In the spirit world, the astral world, they correspond roughly to the position occupied by monkeys in the human world. Monkeys are irresponsible, mischievous, frequently spiteful and vicious, and they have no great reasoning power of their own. They are, as one might say, just animated lumps of protoplasm. Elementals, occupying about the same status in the astral world as monkeys in the human world, are forms which move about more or less without purpose, they jibber and put on strange horrifying expressions, they make threatening motions at an astral traveling human, but, of course, they can do no harm. Always keep that in mind; they can do no harm. If you have ever been so unfortunate as to go to a mental hospital and see really bad cases of mental derangement, you will have been shocked at the manner in which some of the worst cases there come up to one and make threatening, or possibly meaningless, gestures. They slobber and drool, but if they are faced with determination they, being of a very inferior mentality, always retreat.

When you move through the lower astral planes you may meet some of these people, some of these strange, outlandish creatures. Sometimes if a traveler is timid, these creatures cluster around and try to fluster one. There is no harm in that, they are quite harmless, really, unless one is afraid of them.

When you are starting astral travel, you will often get two or three of these lower entities congregating nearby to see how you make out, in much the same way as a certain type of person always likes to look at a student driver taking a car out for the first time. The spectators always hope that something gory or exciting will happen, and sometimes if the student driver is flustered, he or she will collide with a lamp post or something else to the great delight of the spectators. Spectators, as such, mean no harm, they are just sensationalists trying to get a cheap thrill. So with the elementals, they are merely out for cheap entertainment. They like to see the discomfiture of humans, therefore, if you show any fear, these elementals will be delighted and will keep up their gesticulations, their fierce and threatening approaches. Actually, they can do nothing whatever to any human, they are more like dogs who can only bark, and a barking dog does no harm. Furthermore, they can only annoy you so long as you, through your fear, permit them to.

Have no fear, nothing whatever can happen to you. You leave your body, you soar into the astral plane, and about ninety or ninety-nine times out of a hundred you will not see any of these low entities. Again, you will only see them if you are afraid of them. Normally you will soar up and beyond their realm, they are clustered right at the bottom of the astral plane in much the same way as worms cluster at the bottom of a river or sea.

When you move up into the astral planes you will meet many remarkable occurrences. You may see in the distance great and brilliant gleams of light. These are from planes of existence presently beyond your reach. Remember our keyboard? The human entity, while in the flesh, can be aware of only three or four notes, but in getting out of the body and into the astral world you have extended your range of notes a little upward, you have extended that range enough to become aware that there are greater things ahead of you. Some of these things are represented by the bright lights which are so bright that you cannot really see what they are.

But let us content ourselves for the time being with the middle astral. Here you can visit your friends or relations, you can visit the cities of the world and see the great public buildings, you can read books in strange languages, for, remember, in the middle astral plane all languages are known to you. You will need to practice astral travel. Here is a description of what it is like, a description which can be your own experience with practice.

• • •

The day had grown old and the shadows of night had fallen, leaving the purple twilight which gradually grew darker and darker until at last the sky turned indigo, and then black. Little lights had sprung up all around, the whitish-blue lights which illumined the streets, the yellowish lights which were the lights within the houses, perhaps they had been tinted somewhat by the blinds or curtains through which they shone.

The body was resting in bed fully conscious, fully relaxed. Gradually there came a faint creaking sensation, a feeling as if something was drifting, shifting. There was the faintest of faint itches throughout the body, gradually there came a separation. Above the prone body, a cloud formed at the end of a gleaming silver cord, the cloud started as an indistinct mass something like a big blot of ink floating in the air. Slowly it formed into the shape of a human body, it formed and rose to about three or four feet where it swayed and twisted. Over some seconds the body of the astral rose higher, then the feet tilted. Slowly it sank down so that it was standing at the foot of the bed looking at the physical body which it had just left and to which it was still attached.

In the room the flickering shadows crept into the corners like strange animals at bay. The silver cord was vibrating and shining with a dull silvery-blue light, the astral body itself was limned with blue light. The figure in the astral looked about and then looked down upon the physical body resting comfortably on the bed, eyes were now shut, the breathing was quiet and shallow, there was no movement, no twitching; the body appeared to be resting comfortably. The silver cord did not vibrate, therefore there was no evidence of any unease.

Satisfied, the astral form silently and slowly rose up into the air, passed through the ceiling of the room and through the roof above, and out into the night air. The silver cord lengthened but did not diminish in thickness. It was as if the astral figure was a gas-filled balloon tethered to the house which was the physical body. The astral figure rose until it was fifty, a hundred, two hundred feet above the rooftops. There it stopped, floated idly, and looked about.

From houses all along the street and from streets beyond there were the faint blue lines which were the silver cords of other people. They extended up and up, and disappeared into some illimitable distance. People always travel by night whether they know it or not, but only the favored ones, the ones who practice, come back with the full knowledge of all that they have done.

This particular astral form was floating above the rooftops, looking about, deciding where to go. At last it decided to visit a land far, far away. Upon the instant of decision it started into fantastic speed, whirling almost with the speed of thought across the land, across the seas, and as it crossed the sea below, the great waves leapt up with white crests at the top. At one point in its journey, it peered down at a great liner racing across the turbulent sea with all lights on and the sound of music coming from the decks. The astral form sped on, overtaking time. The night gave way to the evening before; the astral form was catching up on time, night gave way to evening, and evening, in its turn, was overtaken and became late afternoon. Late afternoon was outstripped and became noon itself. At last in the bright sunlight the astral figure saw that which it had come to see, the land so far away, a dearly beloved land with dearly beloved people. Gently the astral figure sank to the earth and mixed unseen, unheard among those who were in the physical body.

Eventually there came an insistent tugging, a twisting of the silver cord. Far far away in a different land the physical body which had been left behind was sensing the break of day and was recalling its astral. For some moments the astral lingered on, but at last the warning could no longer be ignored. Up into the air rose the shadowed form, poised motionless for a moment like a homing pigeon, then sped across the skies, flashing across land, across water, back to the place of the rooftop. Other cords were trembling too, other people were returning to their physical bodies, but this particular astral form sank down through the rooftop and emerged through the ceiling over the slumbering figure of its physical. Lightly, slowly, it sank down and positioned itself precisely above the physical body. Slowly, gently, with infinite care, it descended and merged into that physical body. For a moment there was a sensation of intense cold, a sensation of dullness, of leaden weight pressing down. Gone was the lightness, the feeling of freedom, the bright colors experienced in the astral body; instead there was cold. It felt as if a warm body was putting on a wet suit of clothes.

The physical body stirred and the eyes opened. Outside the windows the first faint streaks of daylight were showing above the horizon. The body stirred and said, "I remember all my experiences of the night."

• • •

You, too, can have such experiences; you, too, can travel in the astral, you can see those whom you love, and the greater the ties between you and those you love the more easily you can travel. It needs practice and more practice. According to old Eastern tales, in the days of long long ago all people could travel in the astral but because so many people abused that privilege it was taken away. For those who are pure in thought, for those who are pure in mind, practice will bring release for the leaden, cloying weight of the body, and will enable you to go wherever you will. You will not do it in five minutes, nor in five days. You must imagine that you can do it. Whatever you believe you are, that you are. Whatever you believe you can do, that you can do.

If you really believe, if you sincerely believe that you can do a thing, then you can do that thing. Believe, believe, and with practice you will travel in the astral. Again, have no fear for while in the astral no one can harm you no matter how fearsome, no matter how terrifying is the aspect of lower entities whom you may, but probably will not, see. They can do nothing to you unless you are afraid. The absence of fear ensures your absolute protection. So will you practice, will you decide where you are going? Lie down upon your bed, you must be alone in your bed, of course, and tell yourself that this night you are going to such-and-such a place to see so-and-so, and when you awaken in the morning you will remember everything that you did. Practice is all that is necessary to make this attainable.

Lesson
Eleven

THE SUBJECT OF astral traveling is, of course, of vital importance, and for that reason it might be advantageous to devote this lesson to more notes about that quite fascinating pastime.

We suggest that you carefully read this lesson, go through it at least as meticulously as you have gone through the other lessons, and then decide upon an evening a few days ahead as the evening of your experiment. Spare yourself by thinking that upon the chosen evening you are going out of the body and remain fully conscious, fully aware of all that is happening.

As you know, there is a very great deal in preparing, in deciding in advance what one is going to do. The Ancients of Old used incantations, in other words, they repeated a mantra (that is, a form of prayer) which had as its objective the subjugating of the subconscious. By relating their mantra the

conscious—only one tenth of us—was able to send an impera-
tive order to the subconscious. You could have a mantra such
as this:—

"On such-and-such a day I am going to travel in the astral
world, and I am going to remain fully aware of all that which
I do and be fully aware of all that which I see. I shall remember
all this and recall it fully when I am again in my body. I shall
do this without fail."

You should repeat this mantra in groups of three, that is,
you should say it, then having said it you should repeat it,
then having repeated it you should affirm it once more. The
mechanics of it is something like this: You state a thing, that
is not enough to alert the subconscious because you are
always stating things, and I am sure that the subconscious
thinks that the conscious part of us is very talkative. Having
stated your mantra once, the subconscious is not at all alerted.
The second time the same words are stated, and they must be
stated quite identically, the subconscious begins to take notice. At the third affirmation the subconscious—as one might
say—wonders what it is all about and is fully receptive to your
mantra, and the mantra is received and stored. Supposing you
say your three affirmations in the morning, then you will want
to say them (when you are alone, of course) at midday and
again in the afternoon and again before you retire and go to
sleep. It is as knocking in a nail; you have your nail, you start
the point in the wood but one blow is not enough, you have
to keep administering blows until the nail is in the wood to
the depths desired. In much the same way, the affirmations
administer blows which drive the desired statement to the
awareness of the subconscious.

This is not a new device by any means, it is as old as
humanity itself, for the old old people of days long gone knew
a lot about mantras and affirmations, it is only we in this
modern age who have forgotten, or perhaps have become
cynical about the whole affair. For that reason we impress

upon you the urge that you must state your affirmations to yourself and not let anyone else know about them, for if other skeptical people know about them they will laugh at you and perhaps throw doubt in your mind. It is people laughing and throwing doubt which has stopped adults from seeing Nature Spirits and being able to converse telepathically with animals. Remember that.

You will have decided upon the evening of a suitable day, and when the day in question arrives, you must make every effort to remain tranquil, to remain at peace with yourself and with everyone else. This is of vital importance. There must be no conflict within you that would cause you to become excited. For example, suppose you have a heated argument with someone that day, then you will be thinking of what you would have said if you had had more time to think, you will think of things said to you, and your whole attention will not be focused upon traveling in the astral. If you are disturbed or distressed during the proposed day, postpone your astral traveling consciousness until another more peaceful day.

Assuming that everything is tranquil and that all day you have been thinking of astral traveling with pleasurable anticipation—just as you would pleasurably anticipate a journey to some loved one who lived far away that it would be an event to so travel—then go to your bedroom, undress slowly keeping quite calm and breathing steadily. When you are ready, get into your bed, make sure that your night attire is quite comfortable, that is, it should not be tight around the neck nor should it be tight around the waist, for if you have distractions (such as a tight neckband or a tight waistband), this irritates the physical body and may cause a jerk at a crucial moment. See that your bedroom is of a temperature most convenient to you, that is, neither too hot nor too cold. If you have little clothing on the bed so much the better because you do not want to be oppressed by an excessive weight of material above you.

Turn out your bedroom light, and you will, of course, have made sure that your curtains are drawn closed so that no vagrant rays of light can flicker into your eyes at the wrong moment. With all this satisfactorily accomplished, lie down comfortably.

Settle yourself, let yourself go limp, let yourself become completely and utterly relaxed. Do not fall asleep if you can help it, although if you have repeated your mantra successfully sleep will not matter because you will still remember. We advise you to stay awake if you can because it really is interesting, this first trip out of the body.

Lying comfortably—preferably on your back—imagine that you are forcing another body out of yourself, imagine that the ghostly form of the astral is being pushed out. You can feel it rising up something like a cork rising up through water, you can feel it withdrawing from your own flesh-body molecules. There is a very slight tingling, then will come a moment when the tingling almost ceases. Be careful here because the next motion will be a twitch unless you are careful, and if you do twitch violently your astral body will come back with a thud into the physical.

Most people, in fact we might almost say everyone, has had the experience of apparently falling just at the point of sleep. Learned pundits have stated that this is a relic of the days when humans were monkeys. Actually, this sensation of falling is caused by a twitch which causes the newly floating astral body to fall back into the physical body. Often it will jerk one into complete awakeness, but whatever it is, there is usually a violent twitch or jerk and back comes the astral body without having got more than a few inches out of the physical.

If you are aware that there is a possibility of a twitch, then you will not twitch, so let yourself become aware of difficulties then you can overcome them. After the slight tingling stops make no movement at all, and there will be a sudden coolness, a feeling as if something has left you. You may have an impression that there is something just above you, as if, to put it crudely, someone was dropping a pillow on you. Do not be disturbed, and if you are not disturbed, the next thing you will know is that you are looking at yourself from perhaps the end of the bed, or even from the ceiling looking down. Examine yourself with as much composure as you can manage on this first occasion because you never see yourself so plainly as you do on this first excursion. You will look at yourself, and no doubt you will exclaim with astonishment when you find that you are nothing like you expected. We know that you look in mirrors, but a person does not see a true reflection in even the best mirror. Lefts and rights are reversed, for example, and there are other distortions. There is nothing like coming face to face with yourself!

Having examined yourself, then you should practice moving about the room, look in a closet or in a chest of drawers, observe how easily you can go anywhere. Examine the ceiling, examine those places where you cannot normally reach. No doubt you will find much dust in the inaccessible places, and that will give you another useful experiment; try to leave fingerprints in the dust, and you find you cannot. Your fingers and your hand and your arm as well sink through the wall without any sensation whatever.

When you are satisfied that you can move about at will, look between your astral and your physical. Do you see how your silver cord is sparkling? If you have ever visited an old blacksmith's shop you will be reminded of the way in which the red hot metal sparkled when it was hit by the blacksmith's hammer, but in this case, instead of sparkling cherry-red, the sparklings will be blue or even yellow. Move away from your physical body and you find that the silver cord stretches without any effort, without any diminution of diameter. Look again at your physical body, and then go to where you had planned, think of the person or of the place, and make no effort whatsoever, just think of the person and the place.

Up you will rise through the ceiling, you will see your home and your street beneath. Then, if it is your first conscious trip, you will proceed fairly slowly to your destination. You will be going slowly enough to recognize the terrain beneath you. When you are used to astral traveling consciously, you will go with the speed of thought, and when you can do that there is no limit whatsoever to where you go.

When you are practiced in astral traveling, you can go anywhere at all, not merely anywhere on this Earth. The astral body does not breathe air, and so you can go into space, you can go to other worlds, many people do. Unfortunately, through present day conditions, they do not remember where they go. You, with practice, can be different.

If you find it difficult to concentrate upon the person whom you propose to visit, it is suggested that you have a photograph of that person,—not a framed photograph because if you have a framed photograph in bed you may roll over and break the glass, thus causing cuts. Have an ordinary unframed photograph, and hold it in your hands. Before turning out the light, take a long long look at the photograph, then extinguish the light and try to retain a visual impression of the person whose features are in that photograph. That may make it easier for you.

Some people cannot do astral traveling if they are comfortable, if they are well fed or warm. Some people can only go astral traveling consciously when they are uncomfortable, when they are cold or hungry, and it is indeed a fact, though an astonishing one, that certain people deliberately eat something that disagrees with them so that they get indigestion! Then they can do astral traveling without any particular difficulty. We suppose the reason is that the astral body gets heartily sick of the discomfort of the physical body.

In Tibet and India there are hermits who are walled up, who never see the light of day. These hermits are fed perhaps once every three days, and fed just enough in order that life may be sustained, in order that the feebly flickering flame of life may not be extinguished. These men are able to do astral traveling all the time, and they travel in astral form to anywhere where there is anything to be learned. They travel so that they may converse with those who are telepathic, they travel that they may perhaps influence things for good. It is possible that in your own astral travels you will come across such men as these, and if you do, you will indeed be blessed, for they will stop and give you advice and tell you how you may progress further.

Read and reread this lesson. We repeat again that only practice and faith are necessary in order that you, too, may travel in the astral and be freed for a time from the troubles of this world.

Lesson Twelve

IT IS SO MUCH easier to engage in astral traveling, clairvoyance and similar metaphysical pursuits if a suitable foundation is prepared first. Metaphysical training needs practice, considerable, constant practice. It is not possible to read a few printed instructions and then immediately without practice to go off on a far far journey in the astral. You must practice constantly.

No person would expect a garden to grow unless the seeds were planted in suitable ground. It would be most unusual for a beautiful rose to grow out of a granite rock. Wherefore it appears that you cannot expect clairvoyance, nor any occult art whatever, to bloom where the mind is closed and sealed, where the mind is a constant jangle of ill-connected thoughts. We are later going to deal more exten-

sively with quietude because the present-day clutter of irrelevant thoughts and the constant blare of radio and television
really is stilling metaphysical talents.

The Sages of old exhorted, "Be still and know that I am
within." The old sages devoted almost a lifetime to metaphysical research before committing a single word to paper. Again,
they withdrew into the wilderness, into a place where there
was no noise of so-called civilization, where they were free of
distractions, where no one could drop a bucket or a bottle.
You have the advantage that you can take much benefit from
the lifetime experiences of the ancients, and you can take
advantage of all this without having to spend most of your life
in study. If you are serious, and if you were not serious you
would not be reading this, you will want to prepare yourself,
to make yourself ready for the speedy unfolding of the spirit,
and the best way to do it is to relax first.

Most people have no idea of what is meant by the word
relax. They think if they slump in a chair that is good enough,
but it is not. To relax you must let the whole of your body
become pliant, you must make sure that all muscles are without tension. You cannot do better than to study a cat, see how
the cat completely lets go. The cat will come in, turn round
a few times, and then flop down into a more or less shapeless
heap. The cat does not bother at all about wondering if a few
inches of leg is showing, or if one is looking ungraceful; a cat
comes in to rest, to relax, and relaxation is thus the only
thought in the cat's mind. A cat can flop down and be instantly
asleep.

Probably everyone knows that a cat can see things which
humans cannot. That is because the cat's perceptions are
higher up on our "keyboard," and thus it can see into the astral
at all times, and a journey in the astral for a cat is no more
than it would be for us to cross the room. Let us, then, emulate
a cat because then we shall be on firm ground, and we can

build our structure of metaphysical knowledge on a sound and enduring basis.

Do you know how to relax? Could you without any further instructions become pliant, able to pick up impressions? This is how we would do it; lie down in any position which is comfortable. If you want to have your legs outspread, or your arms outspread—spread them out. The whole art of relaxing is to be completely and utterly comfortable. It will be much better if you relax in the privacy of your own room, because many people do not like anyone to see them in what they wrongly imagine is an ungraceful attitude, and to relax you have to forget all about conventional grace, and, indeed, all about conventions.

Imagine that your body is an island peopled by very small persons who are always obedient to your commands. You can think, if you like, that your body is some vast industrial estate with highly trained, highly obedient technicians at the various controls and nerve centers which make up your body. Then when you want to relax, tell these people that the factory is being shut down, tell them that your present desire is that they leave you, that they shut down their machines and their nerve centers, and go away for the time being.

Lying comfortably, deliberately imagine a host of these small people in your toes, in your feet, in your knees—everywhere in fact. Picture yourself gazing down upon your body and upon all these little people who are pulling up on your muscles and causing your nerves to twitch. Gaze down upon them as if you were some great figure high, high in the sky, look upon these people, and then address them from your mind. Tell them to come out of your feet, leave your legs, command them to march away from your hands and from your arms, tell them to congregate in the space between your umbilicus and the end of your sternum. The sternum, let us remind you, is the end of the breastbone. If you run your fingers down the middle of your body, between your ribs, you will find that there is a bar of hard material, and that is actually the sternum. Run your fingers down a little further until the material ends. So, between that spot and your umbilicus is the designated spot. Command all these little people to congregate in that space, imagine that you can see them marching up your limbs, up your body in their serried ranks, like workers leaving a busy factory at the end of the day.

In coming to the designated spot they will have deserted your legs and your arms, and so these limbs will be without tension, without feeling even, for these little people are the ones who make your machinery work, the ones who feed the relay stations and the nerve centers. Your arms and legs, then, will be not precisely numb, but without any feeling of tenseness, without any feeling of tiredness. We might say that they will be almost not there. Now you have all your little people congregating in the prearranged space like a lot of factory workers attending a political rally. Gaze upon them in your imagination for a few moments, let your gaze encompass all of them, then firmly, confidently, tell them to get off, tell them to leave your body until you instruct them to return. Tell them to go along the silver cord and away from you. They must leave you in peace while you meditate, while you relax.

Picture to yourself that silver cord stretching away from your physical body out into the great realms beyond. Picture to yourself that the silver cord is like a tunnel, like a subway, and imagine all the rush-hour travelers in a city such as London or New York or Moscow—imagine them all leaving the city at once and going out into the suburbs; think of trainload after trainload taking all these workers away leaving the city comparatively quiet. Make these little people do that to you—it is very easy with practice—then you will be quite without tension, your nerves will no longer be a-jangle, and your muscles will no longer be tense. Just lie quiet, let your mind wander. It does not matter what you think about, it does not matter even if you do not think. Let that go on for a few moments while you breathe slowly, steadily, then dismiss those thoughts in much the same way as you dismissed your "factory workers."

Humans are so busy with their petty little thoughts that they have no time for the greater things of the greater life. People are so busy wondering about when the next sale is held or how many coupons are given free this week or what is happening on the television, that they have no time for dealing with the things that really matter. All these mundane everyday things are completely trivial. Will it matter in fifty years time that so-and-so's were selling dresses below cost today? But it will matter to you in fifty years time how you progress now, for keep this thought in mind; no man or woman has ever succeeded in taking a single penny beyond this life, yet every man and woman takes the knowledge that they have gained in this life to the next life. That is why people are here, and if you are going to take worthwhile knowledge to the other side, or just a useless clutter of unrelated thoughts, is a matter which should engage your earnest attention. So, this course is useful to you, it can affect your whole future!

It is thought—reason—which keeps humans in their very inferior present position. Humans talk about their reason, and say it distinguishes them from the animals; it does—indeed it does! What other creatures but humans throw atom bombs at each other? What other creatures publicly disembowel prisoners-of-war or deprive them of very useful appurtenances? Can you think of any creature except a human who mutilates men and women in such spectacular fashion? Humans, in spite of their vaunted superiority, are in many respects lower than the lowest beasts of the field. That is because humans have wrong values, humans crave after money only, crave after the material things of this mundane life, whereas the things that matter after this life are the immaterial things which we are trying to teach you.

Let your thoughts be switched off now that you are relaxing, make your mind receptive. If you will practice and practice again, you will find that you can switch off the endless empty thoughts which clutter you, and you can instead perceive true realities, you can perceive the things of different planes of existence, but these things are so completely alien to life on Earth—so pleasantly alien, too—that there are no concrete terms with which to describe the abstract. Only practice is needed before you, too, can see the things of the future.

There are certain great souls who can drop off to sleep for a few moments and within minutes can again awaken refreshed, and with inspiration shining from their eyes. These are people who can switch off their thoughts at will, and tune in and pick up the knowledge of the spheres. This also you can do with practice.

It is very very harmful indeed for those who desire spiritual development to engage the ordinary, useless, empty round of social life. Cocktail parties—one can hardly think of a worse pastime for those who are trying to develop. Drink, spirits, and alcohol, impair psychic judgement, they may even drive one into the lower astral where one can be tormented by the entities who delight in catching humans in a stage where they cannot even think clearly. They find it most amusing. But parties, and the usual social round with the senseless chatter of empty minds trying to disguise the fact that their minds are empty, is a painful sight for those who are trying to progress. You can only progress if you keep clear of these shallow-minded people whose greatest thought is how many cocktails they can drink at any given gathering, or who prefer to chatter inanely about other people's troubles.

We believe in the communion of the souls, we believe that two people can remain together physically silent, no words need be said, yet these people commune telepathically by "rapport." The thought of one evokes a response in the other. It has been noted that at times two very old people who have lived together for many years can anticipate the thoughts of each other. These old people, truly in love, do not engage in senseless babble or small talk; they sit together picking up silently the message flowing from one brain to another. They have learned too late of the benefits which come to one from the silent communion, they have learned "too late" because old people are, literally, at the end of life's journey. You can do it while still young.

It is possible for a small group of people, thinking constructively, to alter the whole course of the world's events. Unfortunately it is too difficult to get a small group of people who are so unselfish, so unselfcentered, that they can switch off their own selfish thoughts and concentrate only on the good of the world. We say now that if you and your friends will get together and form a circle, each one of you sitting comfortably at full ease, and facing each other, you can do very great good for yourself and for other people.

Each person should have his or her toes touching. Each person should have his or her hands clasped together. No person should touch another, of course, but each one should be as a separate physical unit. Remember the old Jews, the very old Jews; they well knew that if they were bargaining they should stand with their feet together and their hands clasped because then the vital forces of the body were conserved. An old Jew always got the better of the bargain if he stood in that particular manner and his opponent did not. He did not stand that way through cringing subservience, as many people imagine, but because he knew how to conserve and utilize his body forces. When he had achieved his objective, then he could throw his hands wide and stand with legs apart, no longer need he conserve his forces for the attack, for he was the victor. Having attained his end he could stand relaxed. Many Eastern and Near-Eastern people know this.

If each of you in your group keep your feet and your hands together, each of you will conserve body energy. It is much the same as having a magnet and placing a "keeper" across the poles in order to save the magnetic force, without which the magnet would be just a lump of idle metal. Your group should sit in a circle, all more or less gazing at space in the center of the circle, preferably at a space on the floor because then heads will be slightly tilted down, and that is more restful and more natural. Do not talk, just sit—be SURE you do not talk. You have already decided on the theme of your thoughts so no further talk is necessary. Sit like that for some minutes. Gradually each one of you will feel a great peace stealing in upon you, each one of you will feel as if you are being flooded with an inner light. You will have truly spiritual enlightenment, and will feel that you are one with the Universe. Church services are designed with that in mind. Remember that the early priests of all the churches were quite good psychologists, they knew how to formulate things in order to get desired results. It is known that one cannot keep a whole crowd of people quiet without constant direction, and so there is music and directed thought in the form of prayer. If a priest of any sort is standing where all eyes can focus upon him as he says certain things, then he has gained the attention of every person in the audience or congregation, their thoughts are all directed to a certain purpose. This is an inferior way of doing it, but a way which is necessary for mass production among a people who will not devote the time or energy necessary for greater development on other lines. You and your friends can, if you wish, get far better results by sitting in your little group, and sitting in silence.

Sit in silence, each one of you trying to relax, each one of you thinking of pure things or thinking of the designated item. Never mind about last week's grocery bills which you have not yet paid, never mind about wondering what the next season's fashions are going to be; think, instead, of raising your vibrations so you may perceive the goodness, the greatness, which is in the life to come.

We talk too much, all of us, we let our brains chatter away like machines which have no thought. If we relax, if we

remain alone more and talk less when we are in the company
of others, then thoughts of a greater purity than we can now
imagine come flooding in upon us to uplift our souls. Some of
the old country people who were alone all day had far greater
purity of thought than any person in the cities of the world.
Shepherds, while by no means educated people, had a degree
of spiritual purity which many of the priests of high degree
would envy. That is because they had time to be alone, time
to ponder, and when they were tired of pondering, their minds
would go blank and the greater thoughts from beyond would
enter.

Why not practice for half an hour every day? Practice
sitting or reclining, and remember you must be quite fully at
ease. Let your mind become still. Remember, "Be still and
know that I am God," is one saying. Another is, "Be still
and know the I within." Practice in this manner. Let yourself
remain free of thought, let yourself remain free of worries and
doubts, and you will find that within a month you are more
poised, you are uplifted, you are quite a different person.

We cannot end this lesson without referring once again
to parties and idle talk. In some finishing schools it is taught
that one must make small talk in order to be a good host or
hostess. The idea seems to be roughly that guests must never
be left for one moment in silence in case their own personal
thoughts are so murky that their outlook would become cluttered. We say, on the contrary, that in providing silence we
should be providing one of the most precious things upon
this Earth, for in the modern world there is no longer silence,
there is the constant roar of traffic, the constant shrieking of
aircraft overhead, and over all the insensate blare of radio and
television. This can lead to the fall of mankind once again.
You, by providing an oasis of quiet and peace and tranquility,
can do much for yourself and for others, too.

Will you try for a day, and see how quiet you can be? See
how little you can talk. Say only that which is necessary and
avoid all that which is irrelevant, avoid all that which is merely

senseless gossip and chatter. If you do this consciously and deliberately you will be quite shocked at the day's end at how much you normally say which really does not matter in the least.

We have gone on a lot about chatter and noise, and if you will practice silence you will find that there, too, we are right. Many of the religious orders have orders of silence, many of the monks and nuns are commanded to keep silence, and the authorities do not do this as a punishment, they do it because they know that only in silence can one hear the voices of the great beyond.

Lesson Thirteen

WHO HAS NOT, at some time or other, wondered, "What is the purpose of life on Earth? Is it really necessary to have so much suffering, so much hardship?" Actually, of course, it is necessary that there should be suffering and hardship and wars. We place too much store upon the things of this Earth, we tend to think that there is nothing so important as life on Earth. Actually, upon Earth we are merely as actors upon a stage, changing our clothes to suit the role that we have to play, and at the end of each act retiring for a while, to return to the next act perhaps in different garb.

Wars are necessary. Without wars the world would soon be overpopulated. Wars are necessary in order that there may be opportunities for self-sacrifice and for people to rise above the limits of the flesh in the service of others. We look upon life as it is lived on this world as the only thing that matters. Actually it is the thing that matters least.

When we are in the spirit we are indestructible. We are immune from hardships and illnesses. Thus, the spirit which has to gain experience, motivates a body of flesh and bone— a body which is but a lump of animated protoplasm—in order that lessons may be learned. Upon Earth the body is as a puppet, jerking and twitching to the orders of the Overself who, through the silver cord, commands and receives messages.

Let us look at things in a rather different way for a moment, shall we? A person who comes to Earth for perhaps the first time is a helpless creature, something like a baby, and he is not able to make any plans for himself. Thus, plans have to be made for him by other people. We are not concerned with those who are unevolved, for if you are studying this course it shows that you have reached a stage of evolution in which you are able to plan more or less that which you have to learn. Let us look upon the scene before one comes to Earth.

A person—an entity—has returned to the Overself in the astral planes, has returned from one life on Earth. The entity will have seen all the mistakes, all the faults of that life, and will have decided, perhaps alone, perhaps in company with others, that certain lessons were not learned and will have to be undertaken again. So plans are made whereby the entity will go down into a body once more. A search is made for parents who will afford the necessary facilities for the type of environment now required. That is, if a person has to be accustomed to handling money he will be born to rich parents, or if a person has to rise from "the gutter" he will be born to parents in very poor circumstances indeed. He may even have to be born crippled or blind, it all depends on what has to be learned.

A human on Earth is as a child in a classroom. Think of it in terms of classrooms. A child is in a classroom with a lot of other children. For some reason, this particular child does not do so well, does not master the lessons, and so at the end of the term he makes a very poor showing at the examinations. The teachers decide, on the basis of his general attitude and grades during the term, and the general mess that he has made of the examination itself, he is not fit, not ready to be promoted to a higher grade. Thus, the child goes off on school vacation at the end of term with the unhappy knowledge that when school starts again he is going to have to come back to the same old class.

With the resumption of school activities, the child who was not promoted goes back to learn all the same lessons, to have another chance. But those who studied more assiduously go on and reach a higher grade, and perhaps are treated with more consideration by the teachers because these children are ones who have tried, who have mastered their lessons and who have progressed. The one who was left behind feels selfconscious with the new members of the class, he tends to lord it over them for the time being, to show that although he did not pass into a higher grade it was because he did not want to. If at the end of this term the boy does not show signs of progress, then it may be that the teachers will hold a conference, and they may even decide that the boy is of an inferior mentality and recommend that he be moved to a different type of school.

If children at school are doing well and progressing satisfactorily through their studies, there will come a time when they have to decide what they are going to be in later life. Are they going to be doctors, lawyers, carpenters or bus drivers? Whatever it is, they will have to undergo the necessary studies. A doctor will need to learn different things than would a bus driver, and in consultation with teachers the necessary studies are arranged.

So it is in the spirit world; before a human is born, several months before he is born, in fact, somewhere in the world of spirit there is a conference. The one who is going to enter into a human body discusses with advisors how certain lessons may be learned in much the same way as a student upon Earth will discuss how he or she may study to obtain the desired qualifications. The spirit advisors are able to say that the student about to enter into the school of the world shall become a son or daughter of a certain married couple, or even of an unmarried couple! There will be a discussion as to what has to be learned and what hardships have to be undergone, for it is a sad fact that hardship teaches one more quickly and more permanently than does kindness. It is also worthy of note that it does not at all mean that because a person is at present in a lowly position that that person is lowly in the spirit world. Often a person will be in a menial position in a certain life in order that specified lessons may be learned, yet in the life to be the person may be a high entity indeed.

It is unfortunate that upon Earth a person is judged by the amount of money he or she has, by what his or her parents were, and this, of course, is tragically absurd. It is much the same as judging a school boy, or his progress, by how much money his father has instead of judging the boy by his own progress. We repeat that no one has so far succeeded in taking even one single penny beyond the barrier of death, but all knowledge is taken, every experience undergone is stored and taken away into the life beyond. Thus, those who think that because they have a million or so they are going to get a front seat in heaven, are going to be sadly and unpleasantly mistaken. Money, position, race and color do not matter in the slightest; the only thing that matters is the degree of spirituality that one has reached.

To return to our spirit about to enter into another incarnation, when suitable parents have been found, then, at the appropriate time, the spirit will enter into the forming body of the unborn infant, and with the entering into the body there will become an instant erasure of the conscious memories of the life beyond such entering. It would, of course, be a terrible thing if the baby had a memory of when he was, perhaps, very closely, very intimately related to his mother or his father! It would be tragic and painful if the baby could remember that in the past life he was a great king, and now he is the poorest of the poor. For that reason, among many others, it is an act of mercy that the average person cannot remember his or her past life, but when they once again pass through this life and return to the spirit world everything is remembered.

Many people adhere most rigidly to the old statement "Honor thy father and thy mother." While this is indeed a most laudable feeling, it should be made clear that many many people upon Earth will never again see father or mother when they enter into the spirit world. In the old days it was very necessary that the priests do everything possible to gain the cooperation of parents in order that young men and women did not leave the tribes, because the wealth of tribes in those days rested in the young people. The more numerous the tribe, the more easily could they overcome small tribes. Thus it was that the priests exhorted children to obey the parents, and the parents in particular obeyed the priests.

Let us state quite definitely that we do indeed agree that parents should be honored provided they merit it. We also state that if a parent is overbearing, unkind, or tyrannical, then that parent has rejected and spurned all rights to be honored. There is no need whatever for the slavish obedience which some children give to their parents. Some children are adult and married, and have perhaps lived half a century on their own, yet they still tremble with fear or apprehension when the name of a parent is mentioned. Frequently it leads to a neurosis, and instead of commanding love there is perhaps fear and ill-concealed hatred. Yet these children—perhaps half a century or more of age—feel guilt because they have been brought up with the belief, "Honor thy father and thy mother."

For those so afflicted, we would like to say again quite
definitely, quite emphatically, that if you are unhappy with
your parents you will never see them again in the spirit world.
In the spirit world there is the Law of Harmony, and it is
utterly impossible for you to meet anyone with whom you
are incompatible. Thus, if you are married to a partner and
yours is a marriage of convenience, a marriage which you are
afraid to break for fear of what the neighbors will say, you will
never again meet your partner in the spirit world unless he
or she alters so radically (or if you alter) that you are both
compatible.

We must again repeat, so that there is no possibility of
misunderstanding:—If you and your parents are incompatible,
if you do not get on, if you are not happy together, if you are
not suited to each other, then you will not meet on any other
plane of existence. The same applies to relatives, or husband
and wife. They must definitely be compatible and in complete
harmony before they can meet again. This is one of the reasons
why it is necessary for spirits to have a physical body, that
lessons may be learned, because only in the physical body can
two antagonistic entities be brought into contact so that they
may try to "smooth off the rough edges" and reach mutual
understanding.

Later, in another lesson, we shall deal with the problems
of God or Gods, and of different forms of religious belief.
Humans mistakenly think that they are of the greatest form of
existence. That is quite incorrect, and again it is an idea
fostered by organized religions. Religious thought teaches one
that we are made in the image of God, therefore, if we are
made in the image of God, there can be nothing higher than
us! Actually, in other worlds there are some very very high
forms of life. God is not a benevolent old gentleman who
peers at us kindly through the pages of some book. God is a
very real thing, a living spirit who guides us all, but not
necessarily in the way that we have been taught.

Finally in this lesson think over your own relationship with your parents, or with your partner, or with your relations. Are you happy with them? Are you, really? Or are you living apart? Could you contemplate living with any of these people permanently throughout the rest of existence? Remember when you were at school, there were a number of people in the class with you, there were teachers. You had to pay respect to the teachers but they are not permanently associated with your life, they were temporary measures, people appointed to supervise your education. Your parents also are people whom you have chosen—with their permission in the spirit world—to sponsor and supervize your development. If people sincerely love their parents, and not because some religious teaching tells them they should, then they will indeed have the greatest joy of all in knowing that they will definitely meet their parents on "the other side." Conditions on the other side will be what you here on Earth make them.

Lesson
Fourteen

ALL OF US are anxious to get things done for us, to get things given to us. Probably everyone would admit to having prayed for assistance. It is, of course, a natural thing in human affairs to want the assistance of someone else. Human beings feel insecure alone and want the "God-Father" image or the "Mother" image in order that they may feel protected, may feel that they are one of a great family. But in order that one may receive, one must first give. We cannot receive without giving, for the act of giving—the attitude of opening the mind—makes it possible to be receptive to those who are willing to give what we want to receive.

When we say "give" we do not necessarily mean money although it is usual to give money, because that to most people is what they desire above all else. Money at the present time signifies security from want, relief from the fear of starvation, freedom from the visits of the debt collector! Money can be given, and must be given under certain conditions, but "give" also means to give of oneself, to be willing to be of service to others. We can, and must, give money or goods or assistance or spiritual consolation to those who need them. Again, unless we give we cannot receive.

There is much misconception about "give," "alms," "begging," and similar matters relating to so-called "charity" in the Western world. It seems that people imagine that there is something shameful, something degrading in having to solicit assistance from another. But this is definitely not the case. Money is merely a commodity which is lent to us while upon the Earth, it is a commodity with which we can buy happiness and self-advancement by helping others with that money instead of hoarding it uselessly in some dead stone vault.

This, unfortunately, is the world of commerce where a person's measure is taken by the money that he or she has in the bank and by the outward show he or she makes with that money. The flashily dressed man or the woman who gives for self-satisfaction—to build up a false facade—is neither spiritual nor generous. These people spend selfishly in order to bolster their own egos. In the Western world, a man is judged by how well his wife dresses, what sort of car he drives, what sort of a house he occupies; does he belong to this or that club? Then he must be a man of substance because only those in the millionaire class can belong to that club! Again, this is a world of false values, for—let us repeat it endlessly so that it sinks into your subconscious—no man or woman has ever succeeded in taking even one penny or one pin, or even a spent match beyond the River of Death. All that we can take is that contained within our knowledge, all that we can take is the sum total of our experiences, good and bad, generous and mean, which will be distilled down so that only the essence of those experiences remains. And the man who lived for himself alone upon Earth, although on Earth he was perhaps a millionaire, when he goes to "the other side" he will be a spiritual bankrupt.

In the East it is a common sight indeed for the housewife to go to her door at the close of day and find there the robed monk with his humble begging bowl. This is so much a part of life in the East that every housewife sees to it—no matter how poor she may be—that she has food to spare for the mendicant monk who depends upon her generosity. It is considered an honor to the house that a monk should call for sustenance. But contrary to common belief in the West, a monk is not just a parasite or beggar, he is not a shiftless man who is afraid to work and so lives on the bounty of others. Do you know what it is like, these evening scenes in the East?

Let us assume that we are looking down in the East upon some country such as India where this process of giving to the monks is common indeed, as it was in China and Tibet before the communists seized power. We are, then, looking down on a village in India. The evening shadows are falling and lengthening across the ground. The light is taking. on a bluish-purplish tinge; the leaves of the baobab trees are rustling slightly as the nightwinds come along from the Himalayas. Softly along the dusty road comes a monk dressed in tattered robes, carrying with him all that he possesses in the world. He has his robe, with sandals upon his feet, in his hand he carries his rosary. Slung across his shoulder he has his blanket which serves him as his bed. Other small possessions are tucked into his robe. In his right hand he has a staff—not to defend himself against animals or humans, but that he may push aside brambles and branches which otherwise would impede his progress. He uses it, too, to test the depths of a river before he attempts to ford it.

He approaches a house, as he does so he fumbles in the breast of his robe and produces his well-worn, shiny bowl, a wooden bowl which is aged and worn smooth with use. As he approaches the house the door is suddenly opened and a woman stands respectfully at the entrance with a dish of food in her hands. Modestly she looks down—not gazing at the monk—for that would be an impertinence, she looks down to show that she is modest, demure, and of a good name. The monk walks up to her and holds his bowl with two hands. Of course, in the East one always holds a bowl or a cup with two hands because to hold it with one hand only would show disrespect to the food; food is precious, therefore it is worthy of the attention of two hands. So, the monk holds his bowl teady with two hands. The woman puts in a generous supply of food, and then turns away, no word is exchanged, no glance is given, for to feed a monk is an honor not a burden, to feed a monk is to pay to some small extent the debt which all lay people feel toward those who are in Holy Orders.

The woman of the house feels that she and her house have been paid respect that this, a Holy Man, has called at her door, she feels that tribute has been paid to her cooking, she wonders if some other monk may perhaps have said some kind words about the food which she has provided and this has sent another monk to her door. In other houses, women may be looking rather jealously out from their curtained windows, wondering why they have not been chosen for the monk's visit.

With his bowl filled, the monk slowly turns away still holding the receptacle with two hands, and moves across the road again to the shelter of some friendly tree. There he will sit, as he has sat for most of the day, and have his evening meal, the only meal of the day. Monks do not overeat, they live frugally and have just enough to maintain their strength and their health, but they do not have sufficient to make them become gluttonous. Too much food clogs the spiritual development, too rich food or fried foods impair the physical health, and, if one is to develop spiritually, one should live as the monks live, eat enough but no more, eat plainly that the body may be fed but do not eat richly so that the mind is satiated and the spirit locked in the case of clay.

It should be explained that the monk who has had this food does not necessarily feel overcome with gratitude. Through time immemorial a way of life has arisen in the East, a monk is fed as a right, he is not a beggar, not a burden, he is not a shiftless man nor a parasite.

During the day, before the evening meal, the monk will have been sitting for hours beneath a tree, available to all who come his way, available to all who need his services. Those who need spiritual solace will have come to him for help, as will those who have relations who are ill, or even those who want an urgent letter written. Some, too, come to see the monk, to hear if he has any news of loved ones in some far distant place, for a monk is always on the move, walking from town to town, from city to city, traversing the countryside, crossing the land from border to border. And the monk gives his services free, no matter what is wanted of him, no matter how long the service demanded takes, it is free. He is a Holy Man and an educated man; he knows that many of the villagers who need him and the help that he willingly proffers, cannot pay him, they are too poor, wherefore it is right and just that as he has had to study for his knowledge, and as he brings spiritual consolation to people, he has not the time nor the right to work manually and earn a living. Therefore it becomes the duty, the privilege and the honor that those whom he has assisted shall, in their turn, assist him and pay to some small extent with the food which he has to keep body and soul together.

After his meal the monk will rest awhile, and then, rising to his feet and cleaning his bowl with fine sand, he will pick up his staff and stride off into the night, often traveling beneath the light of a brilliant tropical moon. The monk travels far and fast, and sleeps little. He is a man respected throughout the Buddhist countries.

We, too, should be willing to give in order that we may receive. In the days of long ago it was a divine law that all men should give a tenth of their possessions that good may thereby be wrought. This tenth known as a "tithe," soon became an integral part of life. In England, for example, the churches could levy a tithe on all property, on everything that a person possessed. This money was devoted to the upkeep of the church and provided the stipend of the incumbents of a living. It is interesting to note that some ten years ago in England there were a number of law cases where hereditary landlords made a great commotion in the law courts of the land in order that the tithes imposed by the Church of England should be set aside. The hereditary landlords were complaining that having to pay a tenth of their income was ruining them. Actually, they were being ruined by not giving willingly, for unless one gives willingly, it is better not to give at all.

Nowadays standards are rather different from what they were years ago. No longer do people live on tithes nor do they pay tithes, and that is a pity. It is essential that if one is going to progress spiritually one shall tithe for the good of others—and especially as "for the good of others" brings much good to oneself. In short, we can only progress and be helped if we help others.

We are aware of a number of very hard-headed business men of no great spiritual leaning who willingly give a tenth of their income for the good of others—and, more especially, for their own good. They do it not because they are religious, they do it because of hard commercial experience and the facts of account books have taught them that in thus "casting their bread upon the waters" it comes back to them a thousandfold!

Moneylenders—who in some parts of the world are referred to as financial corporations—are not always noted for spirituality nor for generosity, and it seems to us that if even one of these money-lender-financier people has sufficient faith in tithing then there must indeed be something very profitable in the scheme, and we know that many many hard-headed business people do just this.

The occult laws apply to the unspiritual as much as they do to the spiritual. It does not matter if a person studies a lot and reads a lot of spiritual books; that does not make a person spiritual. He might be just reading and deluding himself into thinking he is spiritual. The matter which he is reading may pass straight through his eyes and vanish into thin air without having once impinged upon the memory cells of his brain, yet this person will refer to himself as "a great soul" and really believe that he is making. progress. Actually, he is usually very self-righteous and very unwilling to help others, even though in helping others he would greatly help himself.

We repeat again that it is right and proper and profitable that a person shall give help to others. Incidentally, it is very helpful to the person who gives!

Tithe means, as we have said, a tenth. It also means a way of life because if one gives one also receives. We have in mind as we write a person who was given much help, much assistance; help and assistance which cost money, time, and specialized knowledge. As fast as one trouble was cleared up for that person other troubles descended like a flock of starlings in a newly seeded field. We said, "In order to receive you must first give." The person was most offended, and gave us to understand that he was most generous and did everything possible to help others as the local newspapers would attest. Our contention is that if a person has to have good deeds reported in the local newspapers, then that person is not giving in the correct way.

There are many ways in which we can give. We can, in addition to devoting a tenth of our income to good work, help others in their spiritual needs, or help them by the necessary consolation when they fall upon evil times. In giving to others we give unto ourselves. Just as a business must have a good turnover in order to prosper, so must we have a good turnover of giving in order that we may receive.

It is useless to pray that something be given to you unless you first show that you are worthy by giving to those who need it. Practice it, practice giving, decide how much you can give, what you can give, and how, and having worked out how and why and when, put it into practice, try it for three months. You will find that at the end of three months you will have profited either spiritually or financially, or both.

Will you study this, and study it again, and remember, "Give that ye may receive," and, "Cast your bread upon the waters."

Lesson Fifteen

IT IS AN OLD CUSTOM throughout the world to store one's "loved treasures" in the attic—treasures which one holds onto for old times' sake. Often they lie half-forgotten in the attic until—probably when one is searching for something else—one goes up those usually difficult stairs and prowls about in the dusty, musty cobweb-laden semidarkness.

Here is the old dressmaker's dummy reminding one irresistibly of the passage of years, for a dress made on that would no longer fit! There may be a case, or more than a case, of old letters. What are they, tied with blue ribbon? Or pink? As one looks about one comes across things which one had almost forgotten, things which revive affectionate memories and revive memories of sad times too.

Do you often prowl about in your attic? It is worth a visit every so often, for some useful things are stored in attics, things which bring back memories; things which add up to one's general knowledge. Problems which confronted us in days gone by may have been swept aside effortlessly by new-found knowledge, by experiences gained—lessons learned—through the passage of the years.

But in this particular lesson we are not going to ask you to go into your attic; we are going to suggest that you come with us, follow us to the winding wooden stairs with the old handrail at the side, go up those creaking wooden stairs which makes one feel that they are going to break through at any moment, but they never do. Come with us into our attic, browse around, for this lesson and the one after will be in the rooms of our "attic". In it we have all sorts of little pieces of information which may not necessarily fit into a separate lesson, but they will be of undoubted interest to you and value. So think about our attic, read on and see how much of this applies to you, how much of it clears up little doubts, little uncertainties which may have nagged at your mind or plagued you for some time.

We browsed about quite a bit while we were preparing this lesson, we poked around in various odd corners, upsetting quite a few theories and raising a lot of dust. We concentrated on the people who concentrate too much. You can work too hard, you know. We are quite aware of the old saying, "A man was never killed by too much hard work," but we maintain that if one works too hard at concentrating, then one travels backward. In our work we frequently get letters from students who say, "But I try so hard, I concentrate and concentrate, and all I get is a headache. I do not get any of the phenomena that you mention!" Yes, that is a little "treasure" that we may stop awhile and examine.

One can often try too hard. It is a quirk of humanity, or, possibly more accurately, a fault of the human brain that if one tries too hard one makes no progress whatsoever, in fact, in trying too hard one sets up what can only be termed as a negative feedback. We all know the stodgy fellow who really plods on through life always trying and trying, and trying far harder then anyone else would but he never gets anywhere, he is always in a state of confusion, of uncertainty. Again, when we overtax our brains we generate an excess charge of electricity that actually inhibits further thought!

You may not be an electronics engineer, but if electronics and electricity were used in the study of human brains, then those studies would be greatly facilitated. The human brain has much in common with electronics. Do you know, for instance, how the ordinary radio tube works? There is a filament which is heated by a battery or from the mains. That filament, being heated, gives off electrons in a completely uncontrolled manner. The electrons flow off, they stream off like a frenzied crowd going to a football match. If these electrons are allowed to roam without being controlled in any way, then they are quite useless in radio or electronics. In a tube we have a glass envelope. The filament is in the envelope and as it gets hot the electrons are radiated everywhere, but that is useless; we want those electrons to be collected on what is known as a "plate" which is in close proximity to the filament. As things are, if there was only the filament and the plate, the process of collecting the electrons would be wild, uncontrollable, there would be distortion of a radio program or whatever it was we were trying to receive. Engineers found that if they interposed what they termed "a grid" between the filament and the plate, and they introduced on to the grid a negative current, then they could control the flow of electrons between filament and plate. So this grid, which is indeed a grid—it is often a wire mesh—acts as what is known as a "grid bias." If one applies too much grid bias, then no electrons will flow from the filament onto the plate, they are all repelled by the grid. By altering the grid bias to a suitable value the control can be as desired.

Back to our brain before you are tired of radio. When we concentrate too much, when we really bend our brains to a problem, we all too frequently apply negative grid bias, which has the effect of inhibiting thought completely. So we must not try too hard, we must be sensible about it, we must at all times remember the old Chinese adage, "softlee, softlee, catchee monkey." We must go about our concentration in such a manner that our brains do not become tired. Do only that which is within your capacity, take the middle way.

The middle way is an Eastern way of life. It means that you do not have to be too bad, but on the other hand you do not have to be too good, you have to be something in between. If you are too bad the police will get you, if you are too good, then you will be a stuffed prig or you will be unable to stay upon this Earth, because it is a fact that even Great Entities who come to this sad world of ours have to take some form of disability, some quirk of character, so that while upon Earth they are not perfect, for nothing perfect can exist upon this imperfect world.

Once again, do not try too hard, try to do a thing naturally, within reason, within your capacity. You do not have to go round offering slavish adherence to anything said by others. Use your common sense, adapt a thing or a statement to suit yourself. We might say, "This is a red cloth," but you might see it differently, to you it might be pink or orange or even a light purple, it depends upon the conditions under which you see that cloth; your lighting may be different from our lighting, your sight may be different from ours. So do not try too hard, nor adhere too slavishly to anything. Use common sense, use the middle way, the middle way is a very very useful thing.

Try this middle way, it is the way of tolerance, the way of respecting the rights of others and of getting your own rights respected. In the East, priests and others study judo and other forms of wrestling, not because the said priests are belligerent, but because in learning judo and similar forms of fighting, one learns to control oneself, one learns self-restraint, and above all one learns to give way in order that one may win. Take judo—in this one does not use one's own strength in order to win a battle, one uses the opponent's strength in order that he may be defeated. Even a very small woman knowing judo can defeat a hulking great brute of a man who does not. The stronger the man, the more fiercely he attacks, the easier it is to defeat him because his own strength causes him to fall more heavily.

Let us use judo (or the strength of the opposition) in order to overcome our problems. Do not tire yourself or wear yourself out, think out a problem that is bothering you, do not evade the issue as do so many people. Many people are afraid to look at a problem, they skirt around the edges of the problem probing tentatively but never getting anywhere. No matter how unpleasant a subject is, no matter now guilty you may feel about a thing, get right down to the root of your problem, find out what it is that troubles you, that frightens you. Then when you have discussed with yourself every aspect of the problem, sleep on it! If you sleep on a thing it will be passed to your Overself who has a much greater understanding than you have, for the Overself is a great entity indeed compared to the human body. When your Overself, or even your subconscious, can examine the problem and come up with a solution it will often pass the solution into your consciousness, into your memory, so that when you awaken you may exclaim with delighted amazement that now you have the answer to what was troubling you and which, from thence on, will trouble you no more.

Do you like our attic? Let us move onto another little treasure which is lying about collecting a bit of dust. It is time that we looked into it, gave it an airing and let it see the light of day once again. What is in this package? Let us open it and see.

Too many people nowadays think that to be truly good is to be truly miserable. They think most mistakenly that one has to go about with a grim, sad face if one is religious. Such people may be afraid to smile, not necessarily because it might crack their face, but it might—which is much worse—crack the facade of their thin veneer of religious belief! We all know of the grim old man who is nearly afraid to smile or is afraid to take the slightest pleasure from life in case he has a miserable time roasting in hell for a moment's lapse from grace!

Religion, true religion, is a joyous thing. It promises us life beyond this Earth, it promises reward for all that we have striven for, it promises us that there is no death, nothing about which to worry, nothing of which to be afraid. There is a fear of death ingrained in most humans. That is because if one remembered the joys of the afterlife, one might be tempted to end this life and go on to happiness. That would be the same as a boy escaping from the classroom and playing truant, which does not lead to progress.

Religion, if we really believe in it, promises us that when we go beyond the confines of this world we shall no longer be in the company of those who truly afflict us, we shall no longer meet those who grate upon our nerves, who sour our soul. Rejoice in religion, for if you have the true religion, it is indeed a thing of joy, and a thing about which one must rejoice.

We must confess, with great sadness, that many people who study occultism or metaphysics are among the worst offenders. There is one cult—oh no, we do not give names— who are perfectly sure that they, and they only, are the Chosen; they, and they only, will be saved to populate their own little heaven. The rest of us—poor sinning mortals no doubt— are going to be destroyed in various heartily unpleasant methods. We do not subscribe to this theory at all, we believe that so long as one believes that is all that matters. It does not matter if one believes in religion or in occultism, one must *believe*.

Occultism is no more mysterious or complicated than the multiplication tables or an excursion into history. It is just learning different things, learning things which are not of the physical. We should not go into raptures if we suddenly discovered how a nerve worked a muscle or how we could twitch a big toe, they would be just ordinary physical matters. So why should we go into raptures and think that the spirits are sitting all around us if we know how we can pass etheric energy from one person to another? Please note that we say etheric energy instead of prana or any other Eastern terms; we prefer when writing a course in a language to adhere to that language.

Rejoice! The more you learn about occultism and about religion the more you will be convinced of the truth of the Greater Life which lies ahead of all of us beyond the grave. When we pass the grave we merely leave our body behind us in much the same way as one can leave an old suit of clothes to be collected by the garbage man. There is nothing whatever to fear in metaphysical knowledge, nor is there anything to fear in religion, for if you have the right religion, the more you learn about it the more convinced you will be that it is *the* religion. Those religions who promise hellfire and damnation if you fall off the straight and narrow path are not doing their adherents a good service. In the old days, when people were more or less savages, it was possibly permissible to wield the big stick and try to frighten some sense into people, but now the outlook should be different.

Any parent will agree that it is much easier to control children by kindness than by constant threats. Those parents who keep threatening to call in a policeman or the bogeyman or to sell their children are the ones who cause a neurosis in the child and, later, in the species. But those parents who can control by firmness and kindness, and have their children living in joy, they are the ones who produce good citizens. We wholeheartedly subscribe to the view that one must have kindness and discipline; discipline should never mean harshness or sadism.

Again, let us rejoice in religion, let us be the "children" of the "parents" who teach with love, with compassion, and with understanding. Let us do away with all the falseness, all the baseness of terror and punishment and eternal damnation. There is no such thing as "eternal damnation," no one is ever discarded, there is no such thing as a person being banished from the Spirit World! Every single person can be saved no matter how bad he or she has been; no one has to be rejected. The Akashic Record, with which we shall deal later, tells us that if a person is so terribly terribly bad that nothing can be done with him for the moment he is merely delayed in his evolution, and is later given another chance to come along with "another round of existence" in much the same way as a child who played about in class, and could not pass the end of term examinations, does not move up to a higher grade with his classmates but is kept back to study the curriculum all over again.

One would not say that a child is toasted over a slow fire or tossed to hungry devils for mastication because he skipped some lesson work or played truant a few times. The teachers assigned to him might talk to him rather more firmly than he liked, but apart from that no harm would come to him, and if he were expelled from that particular school, he would soon have to enter another or be in trouble with the truant officer. So with the humans on Earth. If you mess up this chance, don't be too disheartened, you will always get another. God is not sadistic, God is not out to destroy us but to help us. We do God a grave disservice when we think that God is always on the lookout to tear us to pieces or toss us to the waiting devils. If we believe in God let us believe in mercy, because in believing in mercy we shall have mercy, but let us also show mercy to others!

While we are on this subject let us turn over another box, one which has been collecting a lot of dust because no one in the past seems to have been interested in this particular package. Turn it over and see what it says.

According to the Akashic Record, the Jewish people are a race who, in a previous existence, could not make progress at all. They did all the things that they should not have done, and they left undone the things that they should have done. They gave themselves up to the pleasures of the flesh, they became excessively fond of food, fat oily food so that their bodies became cloyed and clogged, and their spirits were not able to soar into the astral by night but were instead bound by their gross fleshly envelopes. These people whom we now call Jews were not destroyed nor subjected to eternal damnation. Instead they were set off on a fresh round of existence in much the same way as children who play about in class may even be expelled from that school for unruly behavior, and they may set off to a fresh school and start off in a different class. So for the Jews. In the present round of existence are people who are in a round for the first time, and when they come in contact with the Jews they are puzzled, confused, and afraid. They do not understand what is different about a Jew, they sense that something is different, they sense that a Jew has some knowledge which appears to be not of the Earth, and so the man and woman in a round for the first time wonders and fears, and what a person fears they persecute. Thus it is that the Jews, being an old, old race, are persecuted because they are having to work their way through a round once again. Some people envy the Jews their knowledge, their endurance, and again, those things which are envied one tends to destroy. But we are not dealing with Jews or Gentiles, we are dealing with joy in religion; joy, pleasure, makes you learn a thing which you would not learn through terror.

There are—we cannot repeat it too often—no such things as eternal torments, there are no such things as fires which are going to singe your skin off and make you feel awfully hot about the whole affair. Examine your thinking, examine that which you have been taught and think how much more reasonable it is that you should have joy and love in your religious belief. You are not responsible for a sadistic father who is going to beat you up or send you into perpetual darkness. Instead you are dealing with Great Spirits who have gone through all this long before humans were ever thought of; they have been through it all, they know the answers, they know the troubles and they have compassion. So—from our attic treasure we say, "Rejoice in religion," smile about your religion, have a warm feeling about your God no matter what you call Him, for God is ever ready to send down healing waves to you if only you will get this terror, this fright, out of your system.

But now it is time for us to leave this attic of ours and to go downstairs again, those old creaking stairs. But soon—in the next lesson—we shall ask you to rejoin us in the attic once again, for, looking about, we see there are quite a number of little items lying on the floor or on the shelves which will be of interest and, we hope, profit. May we see you in the attic in the next lesson?

Lesson
Sixteen

SO WE MEET AGAIN in our attic! We have cleaned up the place a bit and discovered a few fresh items. Some of them will perhaps shine a little ray of light onto a doubt which you have had for some time. Look at this for a start: here is a letter which we received some time ago. It says—shall I read it to you?

"You write much about fear, you say that there is nothing to be afraid of except fear. In your answer to my question you told me that it was fear that was keeping me back, preventing me from progressing. I am not conscious of fear, I do not feel afraid, so what can the matter be?"

Yes, that is quite an interesting problem! Fear—fear is the only thing that can hold one back. Shall we have a look at it? Sit down a moment, let us discuss this problem of fear.

All of us have certain fears. Some people are afraid of the dark, others are afraid of spiders or snakes, and some of us may be aware of our fears, that is, we have fears which are in our consciousness. But—wait a moment—our consciousness is only a tenth of us, nine tenths of us is subconscious, so what happens if the fear is in our subconscious?

Often we will do things under some hidden compulsion, or we will refrain from doing something because of a hidden compulsion. We do not know why we do a certain thing, we do not know why we cannot do a certain thing. There is nothing on the surface, there is nothing that we can pin down. We act irrationally and if we went to a psychologist and lay on that couch for long, long hours, at last it may be dragged out of our subconscious that we had a fear because of something that happened when we were small babies. The fear would be hidden, hidden from our awareness, working at us, nagging at us from our subconscious, it would be like termites attacking a wooden framed building. The building, to all cursory inspections would appear to be sound, flawless, and then, almost overnight, it would collapse under the influence of those termites. The same happens in the matter of fear. Fear does not have to be conscious to be active, it is most active when it is subconscious because then we do not know that it is there, and, not knowing that it is there, there is nothing we can do about it.

Throughout the lifetime of all of us we have been subjected to certain conditioning influences. A person who has been brought up as a Christian will have been taught that certain things are not done, certain things are distinctly forbidden. Yet people of a different religion, brought up differently, are permitted to do such things. So in looking into the question of fear we have to examine what has been our racial and family background.

Are you afraid of seeing a ghost? Why? If Aunt Matilda was kindhearted and generous, and loved you dearly during her lifetime there is no reason whatever to suppose that she is going to love you less when she has left this life and has gone onto a far better stage of existence. So why fear the ghost of Aunt Matilda? We fear the ghost because it is something alien to many of us, we fear a ghost because it may have been taught in our religion that there are no such things, and that one cannot see a ghost unless one is a saint or an associate of saints, or something. We fear that which we do not understand, and it is worth thought that if there were no passports, no language difficulties, there would be less wars because we are afraid of the Russians, or the Turks, or the Afghanis, or something else because we do not understand them, we do not know what makes them tick, or what they are going to do against us.

Fear is a terrible thing, it is a disease, it is a scourge, it is a thing that corrodes our intellect. If we have certain reservations about something, then we must dig down and find out why. For instance, why do certain religions teach that there is no such thing as reincarnation? One obvious example is this; in the days of long ago the priests had utter power and they ruled people by terror, by the thought of eternal damnation. Everyone was taught that they had to make the best of this life because there would be no other opportunity. It was known that if people were taught of reincarnation they might tend to slack in this life and pay for it in the next. In connection with this, it used to be perfectly permissible in the China of long ago to contract a debt in this life to be paid in the next! It is also worth remarking that China became decadent because the people believed so much in reincarnation that they did not bother much in this life, instead they just sat around taking their canaries out in cages under the trees at night, and deciding that they would make up for it in the next life, this one would be more or less of a vacation! Well it did not work that way, and so the whole Chinese culture became decadent.

Once again, examine yourself, your intellect, your imagination. Give yourself deep analysis and find out what it is that your subconscious is trying to bottle up, what it is that is making you so afraid, so worried, so jittery about certain things. When you dig that out you will find that there are no more fears. It is fear that stops people from doing astral traveling. Actually as we well know, astral traveling is remarkably simple, there is no effort to it, it is as simple as breathing and yet most people fear it. Sleep is almost death, sleep is a reminder of death, a reminder that eventually we shall go off into a deep sleep, and we wonder what will happen to us when death, instead of sleep, claims us. We wonder if during our sleep someone will sever our silver cord and we will be off. That cannot happen, there is no danger in astral traveling, there is only danger in fear, in fear that you know and more danger in fear that you do not know. We suggest again, and again, get down to this problem of fear. That which you know and understand is not fearsome, so get to know and understand what it is that you now fear.

We devoted a lot of time to that little incident, did we not? We must move on, for there is much yet to engage our attention, much yet to be dealt with before we can draw the curtains on this lesson and move on to the next. Look about you, look about in our attic. Does anything in particular attract your attention? Do you see that ornament over there? Out of this world, isn't it? Oh! We may have started something with that saying!

"Out of this world!" There are many sayings in common use which are truly descriptive. Someone might say that he or she has seen something so beautiful that it was "right out of this world." How true that is! When we get beyond the confines of this carbon molecule existence, with all its pains and trials and tribulations, we can hear sounds and see colors and have experiences which are, quite literally, "out of this world." Here are we confined in the cave of our own ignorance, we are confined by the bonds of our own lusts, our own wrong thoughts. So many of us are so busy "trying to keep up with the Joneses" that we have no time to look about us. We have the mundane whirl of existence, we have to earn our living, then there are social obligations. After that we have a certain amount of sleep, so it seems that all our lives are planned in one whirl, one mad rush, there is never time for anything. But—wait a minute—is there any need for all this rush? Can we not arrange somehow to have even as little as half an hour each day, and devote it to meditation? If we will meditate, we can get right out of this world. We can, with a little practice, get into the astral and into the next world. The experience is exhilarating, elevating. When we elevate our spiritual thinking, we increase our rate of vibration, and the higher we can perceive on our "piano scale"—do you remember that scale?—the more beautiful the experiences which we may undergo.

"Out of this world" should be our objective, of course. We want to get out of this world when we have learned our lessons, but not before. Look again at our classroom experiences. Many of us may have been heartily sick of staying in a stuffy classroom on a warm summer's day listening to the droning voice of a teacher churning out stuff which really had no interest for us.

Who wanted to know about the rise and fall of a certain Empire? We felt we should be much better off out in the open, we desired above all things to get away from that classroom, that hot and stuffy room with the dull voice droning on. But we could not do so, if we had just run out, there would have been sure retribution from the teachers. If we had skipped our lessons we should have failed our examinations and instead of passing to another grade, we should have been kept back in that same monotonous classroom with another lot of students who would look upon us as curiosities and dunces because we had failed to make the grade.

Let us not, then, get "out of this world" permanently until we have learned that which we came to learn. We can look forward confidently to joys, to ease and to spiritual perfection when we leave this world for that which is so much more glorious. We should always keep in mind that we are here as one serving a prison sentence under particularly doleful conditions. We cannot see how dreadful this Earth is while we are here, but if you could move out now and look down you would have quite a shock, you would be most unwilling to return. That is why so many of us cannot do astral traveling because, unless one is prepared, it is indeed an unpleasant experience to return, all the joy is the other side. Those of us who do astral traveling look forward to the days of our release, but we also make sure that while we are in "our prison cell" we behave as best we may, for if we do not behave we lose our "remission time."

So—let us do the best we can upon Earth so that when we come to pass from this life we are prepared and ready for the greater things of the life beyond. It is worth the small effort involved in living here.

We seem to be very busy in our attic, shifting items, knocking the dust off some which have been sorted for a long time, but let us move on to the other side of this room, let us look at another little item.

Many people think that seers are always looking at one's aura, always reading one's thoughts. How wrong they are! A person with telepathic ability, or the power of clairvoyance, is not always reading thoughts or examining the aura of friends or enemies. Some of the things we should see would be far too unpleasant, far too unflattering. Some of them would indeed burst the balloon of our own imagined importance! There is too much else to do. We have in mind a certain person who sometimes visits us; she will start a sentence and utter three or four words, and then trail off with, "but I don't have to tell you anything, do I? You know everything by just looking at me, don't you?" That is not so! We could know everything, but it would be morally wrong to do so. Have no fear about seers, occultists, clairvoyants, and others, for if they are of good morals they will not be peering at your private affairs even with your invitation. If they are not of good morals they cannot do it anyway! We want to tell you here that the back street seer who tells your fortune for a trifle has no real "seeing" ability. She is usually a poor old woman who cannot make money in any other way. Probably at some time she had clairvoyant abilities, but you cannot do such things on a commercial basis, you cannot tell a person clairvoyantly things about themselves for money because the mere fact of the passing of money causes the telepathic ability to wane. And the back street seer cannot always "see," yet, if she has taken money, then she must put on some sort of a show. Being quite a good untrained psychologist, she will let you do the talking and will then tell you the things that you told her, and you, being deluded by the term "seer," will exclaim with wonder at how accurately she has told you what you want to know!

Have no fear that clairvoyants are looking at your affairs; would you be happy if you thought that you were busy in your own home, writing a letter maybe, and someone came into your room, peered over your shoulder and read what you were writing? Would you like that person to go through your possessions picking up this and reading that, and getting to know all about you, getting to know all that you had, all that you thought about? Would you like to think that a person was tuning in all the time to any telephone conversation that you had? Of course you would not! Let us say once again that a person of good character does not read your thoughts all the time, and a person of bad character quite definitely has not the ability! That is a law of the occult; a person of bad character is not clairvoyant. You might hear a lot of tales about a person who sees this and that and something else. Discount nine hundred and ninety nine percent of it!

A clairvoyant will always wait for you to tell him or her what you want to discuss. The clairvoyant will not intrude into the privacy of your thoughts or of your aura, not even if you invite that clairvoyant to do so. There are certain laws of occultism which must be adhered to most rigidly, for if one breaks those laws one can be punished in much the same way as one can be punished if one breaks a manmade law on Earth. Tell the clairvoyant what you want to tell—he or she will know if you are telling the truth. We will go so far as to admit that! Tell the clairvoyant whatever you want to, but make sure that you do tell the truth, otherwise you are deluding yourself only and not in any way deluding the clairvoyant!

So—remember once again, a good "seer" will not "read your thoughts" and a bad one cannot!

Now here is another little item which we might look at. It is this—so you don't get on with your marriage partner? Well, that may be the obstacle which you have to overcome on Earth. Let us put it this way; horses are entered in races, and if one horse wins consistently, and apparently has no great effort in so doing, that horse is handicapped. You can look upon yourself as a horse. You may have gone too quickly, too easily through your last lessons, in that case you may be handicapped with a partner who is not suitable for you. Make the best of it while you can, remembering that if your partner is really incompatible with you, then you will never, never come into contact with him or her in the life beyond this Earth. If a man picks up a screwdriver or a hammer that is just a tool which suits the need of a job at hand. The partner can be looked upon as a tool which enables one to do a certain job, to learn a certain lesson. A man may become attached to a screwdriver or a hammer, may become attached to it because it enables him to do a job that he has to do. But you may be sure that a man will not be so attached to his hammer or screwdriver that he will want to take it with him "to the other side."

There is so much said and written about the "glory of humanity," but we are going to say that humans are not the greatest form of life. Humans on Earth, for example, are truly a rather scruffy lot, sadistic, selfish and self-seeking. If they were not they would not be upon this Earth, because people come to this Earth in order that they may learn how to over-come those things. Humans are greater indeed when they get beyond life. But let us again make sure that we understand that if we have an unsuitable marriage partner here, or unsuitable parents, it may be because we planned that as something which we would have to overcome. A person may have a vaccination or inoculation, they may, for instance, deliberately take a dose of smallpox (by way of inoculation) in order that they be protected from a more severe and, perhaps fatal dose later on. So it is that our marriage partner or our parents may have been chosen in order that we could learn lessons from associating with them. But, we do not have to meet them again after we have finished this life; in fact, we cannot meet them if they are incompatible with us, for, we must repeat, when we are on the other side of death we are living in harmony, and if people are not in harmony with us they cannot associate with us. Many of us can indeed take comfort from that!

But the shadows of night are closing in, the day is coming to an end. We feel that we should not detain you any longer for you will have much to do before the night falls. Let us leave the attic and close the door gently behind us, close the door upon all the "treasures" contained therein. Let us descend those aged creaking stairs again, and go our separate ways in peace.

Lesson
Seventeen

HAVE YOU EVER had a person walk up to you bubbling with excitement and then, almost grasping your jacket, burst out, "Oh, my dear! I had a most terrible experience last night; I dreamed that I was walking down the street without a single stitch of clothing on. I was most embarrassed!" This has happened in various forms and various versions to many people. One may have had a dream in which one was suddenly transported to a drawing room fall of elegantly dressed people, and then discovered that one has omitted to put on one's clothing. Or you may have had a dream yourself in which you found yourself standing on some street corner again either in some outlandish garb, or without any garb whatsoever. That can be, you know, that can have been an actual astral experience. Those of us who can see people doing astral traveling have some amazing and amusing encounters. But this course is not a discourse on witticisms, but instead is designed to help you on what is, after all, a perfectly normal occurrence.

Let us devote this particular lesson to dreams, because dreams in one form or another happen to anybody, to everybody. From time immemorial dreams have been looked upon as omens or signs or portents, and there are even those who purport to tell fortunes by one's dreams. Others consider that dreams are just figments of the imagination when the mind is temporarily divorced from controlling the body during the process of sleep. This is quite incorrect, but let us get down to this dream business.

As we have discussed in previous lessons, we consist of at least two bodies. We are going to deal with two bodies only, the physical and the immediate astral, but of course there are many more bodies. When we go to sleep, the astral body gradually separates from the physical body and drifts up from the reclining physical. With the separation of the two bodies the mind is indeed separated. In the physical body there is the mechanism—in much the same way as one can have a broadcasting station, but when the announcer goes off there is no one left to send messages. The astral body, now floating above the physical, ruminates for some moments deciding where to go and what to do. As soon as a decision has been reached, the astral body tilts feet foremost and settles down usually at the end of the bed. Then like a bird leaving a twig, the body gives a little leap upward and is gone, soaring away at the end of the silver cord.

Most people, in the West particularly, are not aware of the actual occurrences of their astral traveling, they are not aware of any particular incident, but when they return they may have a warm feeling of friendship, or they may say, "Oh, I dreamed of so-and-so last night, he did look well!" In all probability the person actually did visit "so-and-so," whoever it was, because such travel is one of the simplest and most frequently undertaken. For some peculiar reason we always seem to gravitate to old haunts, we seem to like to go places where we have visited before. In fact the police have a statement to the effect that criminals always return to the scene of their crimes.

There is nothing at all remarkable in us visiting friends because we all leave the physical body, we all do astral journeying and we must go somewhere. Until one is educated to the subject, one does not roam in astral realms, but instead clings tenaciously to known places on the surface of the Earth. People who have not been taught about astral traveling may visit friends overseas, or a person with a very great desire to see some particular shop or location will go and see the shop or location, but upon their return to the flesh and to awakeness they think that they have had a dream.

Do you know why you dream? We all have experiences which are excursions into reality.Our "dreams" are as real as a journey from England to New York by plane or ship, or from Aden to Agra by similar means, yet we term them "dreams." Before delving further into the subjects of dreams let us remind one that since the convention of Constantinople in the year when the leaders of the Christian Church decided what was to be embodied in "Christianity," much of the teachings of the Great Masters have been distorted or suppressed. We could add some very pungent comments on all this from information we have obtained from the Akashic Record, but our purpose in preparing this course is to help people to know themselves, not to tread on anyone's corns no matter how fallacious those "corns" of belief may be. Let us content ourselves with stating that in the Western hemisphere for several centuries past people quite definitely have not been taught anything about astral traveling because it does not fall into any portion of organized religion. Incidentally, let us remind you that we say here "organized religion!"

Again, in the Western hemisphere most people do not believe in fairies nor in Nature Spirits, and children who see fairies and Nature Spirits, and who undoubtedly play with such entities, are laughed at or scolded by adults who really should know better, for in this, as in many other cases, the child is far more clever and far more awake than is the adult. Even the Christian Bible states that "Unless ye be as a little child you cannot enter into the Kingdom of Heaven." We could state this differently and say, "If you have the belief of a child uncontaminated by adult disbelief you can go anywhere at any time."

Children, being scoffed at, learn to disguise what they really see. Unfortunately they soon lose the ability to see other entities because of this need of concealing their real abilities. It is much the same in the case of dreams. People have experiences when their physical bodies are asleep, for of course the astral body never sleeps, and when the latter returns to the former there may be a conflict between the two; the astral knows the truth and the physical is contaminated and clogged by preconceived notions inculcated from childhood up to adulthood. Through conditioning, adults will not face up to the truth, so there arises a conflict; the astral body has been off and done things, experienced things, seen things, but the physical must not believe in this because the whole teaching of Western people is to disbelieve anything that cannot be held in the two hands and pulled to pieces to see how it works. Westerners want proof, more proof, and still more proof, and all the time they try to prove that the proof is wrong. Thus we have the conflict between the physical and the astral, and that leads to a need for rationalization. In this case the dreams—so-called—are rationalized into some sort of experience, frequently with the weirdest results imaginable!

Let us go into it again; we could have all sorts of unusual experiences when astral traveling. Our astral body would like us to wake up with a clear memory of all these experiences, but again, the physical body cannot permit it, so there is a conflict between the two bodies, and some truly amazingly distorted pictures come back into our memories, things which could not possibly happen. Whenever anything happens in the astral which is contrary to the physical laws of the physical Earth there is conflict, and so fantasy sets in and we get nightmares or the most unusual happenings which one can imagine. In the astral state, one can levitate, float upward, travel anywhere and see anyone, and visit any of the centers of the world. In the physical it is not possible to move across the world in the twinkling of an eye, or even to lift above one's rooftop. Thus it is, we repeat, that in the conflict between the physical body and the astral body there are such extremely distorted renderings of our astral traveling experiences and this nullifies any benefit which is trying to be sent down by the astral. We get so-called dreams which do not make sense to us, we dream all sorts of rubbish, or so we say when we are in the physical, but the things which are rubbish in the physical are commonplace in the astral.

Let us return to our original remarks about walking down the street without a stitch of clothing on. Quite a number of people have had this highly embarrassing experience apparently in a dream, but, of course, it is not a dream at all! It arises from the fact that when one goes astral traveling one may forget all about wearing astral clothes. If a person does not "imagine" the necessary covering then we have the spectacle of someone traveling in the astral completely nude. Many times a person will leave the physical body and soar upward and outward in a great hurry, in great excitement at having got free of the cloying flesh. Getting out of the body was the prime achievement, leaving no opportunity for thinking about other things.

The natural body, we must remind you, is a body without clothing for clothing is a purely man-made convention which has no point in reality. We might digress here for a moment to tell you something else which possibly will intrigue you.

In the days of long ago, man and woman could see the astral of each other. Thoughts then were plain to all, one's motives were absolutely open, and, we tell you again, the colors of the aura flare most vividly and most strongly around those areas which people now keep covered! We now keep certain areas covered because we do not want others to read our thoughts and motives which may not be always desirable. But this, as we said, is quite a digression and has little bearing on dreams, it is a point, though, which may cause you to ponder on clothing.

When one is doing astral traveling one usually "imagines" the type of clothing which one would normally wear in the daytime. If this is omitted a clairvoyant receiving an astral visitor may receive that person and find that he or she has not a stitch of clothing on. We have had people call on us in the astral and they were wearing either nothing or perhaps a pajama jacket, or some other quite "out of this world" garment which defies description and possibly would not be found in any lingerie catalog of the present day. It is a fact also that people who are overly clothes conscious will often imagine themselves—dream themselves up—clothing which they would not at all wear when in the physical body. But all this does not matter, because we again state that clothing is merely a convention of humanity and we do not suppose that when we get to heaven we shall be wearing clothing such as there is upon this Earth.

Dreams, then, are a rationalization of actual living events which occur in the astral world, and as we have previously stated, when one is in the astral one sees with a far greater range of colors and with far, far greater clarity. Everything is brighter, everything is "larger than life," one can see the most minute details, the colors are of a range far surpassing anything that can be upon this Earth. Let us give an example here.

We wandered out in our astral form far across the land and over the sea to a distant country. The day was brilliant with a vivid blue sky, and the sea beneath us had gentle white-topped waves flicking up at us, but, of course, not touching us. We sank down upon a golden sand and stopped to examine the wondrous diamond-like structure. Every point of sand glittered like gems in the sunlight. We moved along gently over waving fronds of seaweed, we were amazed at the delicate browns and greens, and the air bladders which seemed to be turning golden-pink. To our right was a rock of greenish tinge, it looked for a moment as if of the purest jade. We could see part way through the outer surface, we could see the veins and the striations, and we could see also some minute fossil-like creatures which had been embedded in the rock millions of years before. As we moved around we looked about us with eyes that seemed to be new, with eyes that saw as never before. We could see what appeared to be transparent globes of color floating in the atmosphere, globes which were indeed the living force of the air. The colors were marvelous, intense, varying and our acuity of vision was such that we could see as far away as the curvature of the Earth would permit without causing us to lose any detail whatsoever.

Upon this poor old Earth of ours, while encased in flesh, we are comparatively blind, we have a limited range of colors and a poor perception of the shades of colors. We suffer from myopia, astigmatism, and other defects which make it impossible for us to see things as they really are. Here we are almost bereft of senses and perceptions, we are poor things indeed upon this Earth encased as we are in a sheath of clay, loaded down with lusts and grudges and clogged with the wrong type of food, but when we get out into the free world of the astral we can see—see with the greatest clarity—see colors such as we never saw upon the Earth itself.

If you have a dream in which you see with startling clarity, and in which you are delighted by the amazing array of colors, then you can know that you have not had an ordinary common dream, but are rationalizing a genuine astral traveling experience.

There is another matter which prevents many people from remembering their pleasures in the astral. It is this: when one is in the astral, one is vibrating at a far, far higher rate than when one is encased in the body. It is an easy matter when leaving the body, because the difference in vibrations matters not at all when one is going out, the obstacles occur when we return to the body, and if we know what those obstacles are now, we can consciously dwell upon them and help astral and physical vehicles to reach some sort of arrangement.

Let us imagine that we are in the astral, our flesh body is below us. It is vibrating at a certain speed, "ticking over" almost, while the astral body is a-quiver with life, with vitality, for you are not bogged down with illness or with suffering in the astral. Perhaps it will help us if we put things in terms of the Earth. Let us consider that we are dealing with the problems of a person in a bus; the bus is traveling at, maybe, twenty or thirty miles an hour, and the passenger urgently desires to leave the bus, which, unfortunately, cannot be stopped. So the problem is that the passenger has to jump off the bus in such a manner that he alights on the roadway without hurting himself in any way at all. If he is careless, he gets badly damaged, but if he knows how, it can be done easily for one often sees bus personnel doing it. We have to learn by experience how to get off the bus when the vehicle is moving, we also have to learn how to get into the body when the speeds of the two vehicles are different.

When we return from astral traveling experiences, our problem is to get into the body. Again, we are vibrating in the astral at a much higher rate than we are in the physical, and as we cannot slow down the one nor speed up the other more than a very limited amount, we have to wait until we can "synchronize a harmonic" between the two. With practice we can do that, we can slightly speed up the physical body and slightly slow down the astral body so that while they are still at widely dissimilar vibrations, there is a fundamental harmonic—a compatibility of vibration—between the two, and that enables us to "get in" safely. It is a matter of practice, instinctive, racial-memory practice, when we can do that we can get all our memories intact.

Do you find this difficult to realize? Then let us imagine that your astral body is a phonograph pick-up. Your physical body is a turning record turning at, say, 45 rpms. Our problem is to put the needle onto the rotating record so that we hit upon one particular word or musical note. If you think of the difficulties of putting this phonograph pick-up in contact with the record so that the previously determined word or musical note is chosen, then you will appreciate how difficult it is (without practice) to come back from the astral with memories intact.

If we are clumsy or unpracticed, and we come back without being in synchronization we awaken feeling thoroughly out of sorts, we feel cross with everything; we may have a migraine, possibly we feel sick and bilious. That is because the two sets of vibration were united with a clash just as one can get disharmony and a very definite clash if one changes gears in a car in a clumsy manner. If we come back at the wrong rate of vibration we may find that the astral body does not fit exactly into the physical body, it may be tilted to one side or the other and the result is thoroughly depressing. If we are so unfortunate as to do this, the only cure is to go to sleep again or rest as quietly as possible, not moving, not thinking if one can manage it, keeping quite still and trying to get the astral body free from the physical once more. The astral body will drift up and lift a few feet above the physical body, and then, if we allow it, it will sink down and come back into the physical body in perfect alignment. We shall not feel sick or depressed any more. It only takes practice and perhaps ten minutes of your time. It is better to give this ten minutes and feel well, than jump up all in a rush and feel that you would be happy to die on the spot, because you cannot and will not feel better until you have been to sleep again and allowed your two vehicles to come completely into alignment.

Sometimes one comes back to awareness in the morning with memories of a very peculiar dream indeed. Possibly it may be of some historical occurrences, or it may be quite literally something "out of this world." In that case, it may well be that for some specific reason connected with your training you have been able to contact the Akashic record (we shall deal with that in a later lesson), that you could see what happened in the past, or, more rarely, what will probably happen in the future. Great seers who make prophecies can often move the future and see probabilities, not actualities, for they have not happened, but probabilities can be known and foretold. You will see from this that the more one can cultivate a memory of what occurs in the astral, the more benefits one can derive because there is no point in learning something with much toil and trouble if one is going to forget all about it within the next few minutes.

It frequently happens that one awakens in the morning thoroughly bad tempered, thoroughly hating the world, and all that is within it. It takes one many, many hours to recover from this really black and gloomy mood. There are a number of reasons for this particular attitude; one is that in the astral state one can do pleasant things, go to pleasant places and see happy people. Normally one goes into the astral as a form of recreation for the astral body while the physical body sleeps and recuperates. In the astral, one has a feeling of freedom, an utter lack of restriction and constriction, the feeling is truly wonderful. And then comes the call back into the flesh to start another day of what? Suffering? Hard work? Whatever it is, it is usually unhappy. And so having come back, having been torn away from the pleasures of the astral, one is truly unhappy and bad tempered on awakening.

Another reason, and not such a pleasant one, is that when we are on Earth we are as children in a classroom learning, or trying to learn, the lessons which we ourselves planned to learn before coming to the Earth. When we go to sleep it is so that the astral body can "leave school" and go home at the end of the day in just the same way as children return to their homes at the end of the day. Many times, though, a person who is self-satisfied and complacent upon the Earth, thinking that he or she is a very important person, will go to sleep and then awaken in the morning in a thoroughly bad mood. This is usually because that person has seen in the astral that he is making a shocking mess of his life on the physical Earth, that all the smugness and all the complacency is not really getting him anywhere. It does not at all follow that because a person has a load of money and acres of property that he is doing a good job. We come to Earth to learn specific things, just as a person going to a school or college learns to do specific things. It would be quite useless, to give you an example, for a college student to enroll for a course leading to a doctor of divinity degree and then for no explainable reason find that he was going to collect all the trash, all the garbage, from some local town. Too many people will think that they are doing extraordinarily well because they are amassing money by swindling other people, by overcharging, by generally profiteering and giving "bad deals." Those people who are class conscious or the *nouveau riche* are not really proving anything except that they are making a resounding failure of life upon Earth. There is a time when everyone has to face up to reality, and reality is not upon this Earth, for this is the world of illusion wherein all values are wrong, where for purposes of tuition one believes that money and temporal power and position are all that matters. Nothing could be further from the case than this, for the mendicant monks of India and elsewhere are of more spiritual value to future life than the high-powered financier who lends out money at exorbitant interest to poor people who are hard-pressed and really suffering. These financiers (really they are money-lenders) really wreck the homes and futures of those who are so unfortunate as to fall behind with one of the extortionate payments.

Let one of these high-powered financiers and others of their ilk go to sleep, and assume that for some particular reason they can get free from the flesh and get far enough to see what sort of a mess they are making. Then they come back with a perfectly shocking memory, they come back with an awareness of what they really are and with a determination that they will "turn over a new leaf." Unfortunately when they come back into the physical, being of a low type anyway, they cannot remember and so they just say that they have had a disturbed night, they shout at their subordinates and generally bully everyone in sight. And so they give way to "Monday morning blues," but sadly enough they do not let this occur on Monday morning only but almost every other day!

"Monday morning blues." Yes, that really is the case, and for a special reason. Most people have to work fairly regularly, or at least put in regular hours of work during so many days a week; at the end of the week there is a period of relaxation, a change of vocation and often of venue. People sleep more peacefully at the end of the week and so the astral body goes out and travels further, it goes up to where perhaps it can see what sort of a job the physical is doing on Earth, and then when it returns so that the physical body can start work on Monday morning there is generally much gloom. This is the cause of "Monday morning blues."

Yet another class of people should engage our attention even if for a few moments only; those who sleep little. These people are unfortunate enough to have so much on their astral conscience that the astral body is not at all willing to leave the physical and go out and face up to things. Often a drunkard will be afraid to fall asleep because of the quite interesting entities which gather around his emerging astral body. We have already dealt with "pink elephants" and other fauna and flora of that type.

The physical, in such a case, will stay awake and be the cause of much suffering in the physical and on the astral. You have probably known people who are on edge all the time, they are on the move all the time, they are "jittery" and cannot rest for a moment. All too frequently these people are those who have so much on their minds—on their consciences— that they just dare not rest in case they start to think and realize what they are, and what they are doing, and what they are undoing. So the habit starts—no sleep, no relaxation, nothing which gives the Overself an opportunity of really getting in touch with the physical. These people are like a horse which has taken the bit between its teeth and is bolting wildly down the road to the danger of all. If people cannot sleep, they cannot profit by a life on Earth, and not profiting in this life, then they have to come again to do a better job next time.

Do you wonder how to decide whether a dream is a figment of the imagination or is a distorted memory from an astral journey? The easiest way is to ask yourself, do you see things with greater clarity in that dream? If you do, then it is a memory of astral traveling. Were the colors more vivid than you can remember seeing them upon Earth? Then, again, it is astral traveling. Often you will see the face of a loved one, or have a strong impression of a loved one; that is because you may have visited that person by astral traveling, and if you go to sleep having in front of you a photograph of the loved one, then you can be sure that you are going to travel there when you close your eyes and let yourself relax.

Let us take the other side of the coin. You may have awakened in the morning ruffled and not a little angry, thinking of some particular person with whom you are definitely not in harmony. Perhaps you went to sleep thinking of that person, thinking of some dispute, some wrangle with which you and he were engaged. You may have visited him in the astral, and he, also in the astral, discussed with you a solution to the problems. You may have settled the matter, you may both have determined in your astral states that upon Earth you would remember the solution and you would come to an amicable agreement. Or, on the other hand, the battle may have been of even greater intensity so that when you came back to the Earth you had even greater antipathy to each other than before. But no matter whether you had an amicable arrangement or not, if, in coming back to the physical, you had a bad jerk or did not synchronize yourself with your physical body, then all your good intentions, all your good arrangements would be shattered and distorted, and upon awakening your memory would be of disharmony, dislike, and bitter frustrated rage.

Dreams—so-called—are windows into another world. Cultivate your dreams, examine them, when you go to sleep at night decide that you are going to "dream true," that is, decide that when you awaken in the morning you will have a clear and uncontaminated memory of all that happened in the night. It can be done, it is done, it is only in the Western world where so much doubt, so many shouts for proof are heard, that people find it difficult. Some people in the East go into trance which, after all, is only one method of getting out of the physical. Others fall asleep, and when they awaken they have the answers to the problems which perplexed them. You, too, can do this, you, too, with practice, and with a sincere wish to do it only for good can "dream true" and open wide that window into a most glorious phase of existence.

Lesson
Eighteen

WE HAVE KNOWN each other for some time now through the medium of this course. Perhaps we should pause a while to take stock of our position and look about us, and think of what we have read and presumably what we have learned. It is essential to stop every so often for the purpose of recreation. Do you ever think that recreation is really "re-creation?" We mention this point because it is all tied in with tiredness; if one becomes tired one cannot do one's best work. Do you know what happens when you get tired?

We do not have to have great knowledge of physiology in order to understand why we get stiff and sore if we overtax a muscle. Let us consider that we have been repeating a certain action, perhaps lifting a heavy weight with the right arm. Well, after a time the muscles of the right arm begin to pain us, we get a most peculiar sensation in the muscles and if we continue too long we suffer real pain instead of just soreness. We should look into this even closer.

During this course it has been stressed that all life is electrical in origin.Whenever we think we generate an electric current, whenever we move a finger even, we send an electric current in the form of a nerve impulse which "galvanizes" a muscle into action. But let us consider the arm which we have abused with overwork; we have been lifting something too often for too long and the nerves which carry the electric current from the brain have become overstressed. In much the same way, if we get an ordinary house fuse and overload it, the fuse may not immediately blow but instead it will show evidence of overload in that it becomes discolored. So with our nerves leading to muscles, they become overstressed with the passage of continuous current, and the muscles themselves get tired of expanding and contracting continuously.

Why do they get tired? That is easy to answer! When we move a limb, the muscles become stimulated from the brain. The electric current causes secretions to flow in the muscular structure which causes the strands of muscles to strain apart, so that if you get a whole strand, or collection of strands, straining apart, the result is to decrease the total length, and that means a limb had to bend. That is all right—we are not going into physiology—but a secondary result is that the chemicals involved in causing the striations of muscles to strain apart become crystallized and embedded in the tissue. Thus it is that if we send these secretions, these chemicals, into the musculature more quickly than the tissue can absorb them, the result will be crystals, and those crystals having very sharp edges will cause considerable pain if we persist in our attempts to move the muscles. We can only wait perhaps a day, or two days, until the crystals have been absorbed and the fibers of the muscles are again free to slide smoothly and effortlessly over each other. It is worth noting in passing that when one has rheumatism, one has crystals in various susceptible portions of the body which lock tissue together. Actually, any person with rheumatism can move the afflicted limb, but to do so would cause intense pain because of the crystals lodged in the tissue. If we could find some way of dissolving the crystals, then we should be able to cure rheumatism, but that is not yet.

This is rather taking us away, though, from our original intention to consider some of the things we have learned, or, on second thought, perhaps it is not! If you are trying too hard you will not get anywhere because your brain will become overtired. Many people cannot adopt the middle way because they have been brought up to believe that only the hardest work merits results. People strive and slave, and they get nowhere because they are over-trying. Sometimes people who try so hard become overtired, and then they say horrible things because, quite literally, they are not in possession of their full senses! When we become tired, the electric current produced in the brain fades, it becomes less, and so the negative electricity overrides the positive impulses making us bad tempered. Bad temper is the opposite of good temper, it is the negative aspect of good temper, and if we let ourselves get bad tempered through overtiredness, or through any other cause, it means that we are in effect corroding cells which produce current within us. Do you drive a car? Do you ever look at the battery of your car? If you do, you will at times have seen a most unpleasant greenish deposit around one of the terminals of the battery. In time it will eat away the wires leading from the battery to the car itself. In much the same way, if we neglect ourselves as we had neglected that battery, we find that our own ability becomes seriously impaired and we then have a pattern of bad temper. A wife who started out her married life full of the best intentions might give way to a little nagging doubt about her husband; she will voice those doubts, and by repeating those doubts a few times she will establish a habit, and thus possibly without knowing anything about it she will turn into a nagging wife. Husbands can similarly become just as negative! Keep good tempered; you will keep better health. Do not go in for these slimming fads because the well-padded person is invariably better tempered than the skinny wreck who totters around with almost a rattle of bones!

This matter of the "middle way": it is clear that you should do your best under all circumstances. It is equally clear that you cannot do more than your best and effort beyond this is merely lost effort, which needlessly will tire you out. Look at it as a generating station—we have an electric generating station which is providing light for a certain number of lamps. If the generator runs at such a speed, or provides such an output that the needs of the lamps are easily fulfilled, then the generator is working well within its capacity. But if for some reason the generator is speeded up and the output is far greater than can be absorbed by the lamps, all the excess output has to be shunted off somewhere—wasted—and it also wastes the life of the generator which is running too fast needlessly.

Another way to put it is this; you have a car and you want to go along the highway at, perhaps, thirty miles an hour (most people want to go a lot faster than that, but thirty miles an hour is good enough for our illustration). If you are a sensible driver you will be in top gear just rolling along at thirty miles an hour with the engine rotating quite slowly. At that speed there will be very little wear, and no strain at all, on the engine which is working well within its capacity. But supposing you are not such a good driver and you charge along the highway in low gear at thirty miles an hour. Then the engine may be going five or six times faster because of the gearing and the engine will be putting out perhaps as much power, as much effort, as it would need to do a hundred miles an hour in top gear. So you get a lot of noise, terrific gas consumption, and five or six times as much wear to accomplish the same aim as you would do in top gear. The middle way, then, means taking the sensible course, working just as hard as is necessary to accomplish a specific task, but not frittering away your life and your energy in overworking. Too many people think that they have to work and work and work, and the harder they work to accomplish an objective, the more merit accrues to them. Nothing could be further from the truth, one should always—we cannot repeat it too often—work only hard enough to do the task in hand.

But let us get back to recreation. Recreation, as we have said, is re-creation. If we tire ourselves, it means that only certain muscles, only certain areas, of the body have become tired. If, for instance, we have been lifting our right arm too much, perhaps shifting bricks, perhaps shifting books, then the arm will begin to tire, will begin to ache, but our legs are still in working order as are our ears or eyes. So let us "re-create" ourselves by going for a walk, by listening to good music, or by reading a book. In doing so we shall be using other nerves and other muscles and we shall actually be drawing off any surplus charge of neural electricity from the muscles which have been overstressed and now need to relax. So, in recreation you re-create yourself and your abilities.

Have you been working quite hard trying to see your aura? Trying to see the etheric? Perhaps you have been trying too hard. If you have not had the success which you desire, don't be disheartened, it takes time, patience, and quite a lot of faith, but it can be done. You are trying to do something which you have not done before, and you would not expect to become a doctor or a lawyer or a great artist overnight, you would expect that if you were to become a lawyer you would have to go to school, then to high school, and on to some university. It would take time, it might take years; you would be working conscientiously for many many hours each day, and perhaps many hours each night to attain your objective of being—what?—a doctor? A lawyer? A stockbroker? It all boils down to this; you cannot achieve results overnight. Many of the Indian philosophies tell us that under no circumstances should we try to see clairvoyantly in less than ten years! We do not subscribe to that view at all, we believe that when people are ready to see clairvoyantly, then they will see clairvoyantly, but we do subscribe to the view that they cannot attain results overnight. They have to work for what they are going to get, they have to practice, they have to have faith.

If you are studying to be a doctor, then you have faith in your teachers, you have faith in yourself, you do your lesson work in class, you do your homework when out of class, and still training to be a doctor takes years. When you are studying with us, and trying to see the aura, how long do you study? Two hours a week? Four hours a week? Well, however long it is, you are not studying eight hours a day and doing homework as well. So, have patience because the aura can definitely be seen and will be seen if you have that patience and faith.

We, throughout the years, have had a tremendous amount of correspondence from people all over the world, even from people behind the Iron Curtain. There is a young girl in Australia with marked powers of clairvoyance, she had to hide her abilities because her relatives think that there is something peculiar about her if she says that she knows what they are thinking or if she can discuss the state of their health. There is another lady in Toronto, Canada, who, in a period of just a few weeks, can see the etheric, she can see the etheric power streaming from fingertips, and she can see the lotus flower waving on the top of a head. Her progress has been quite marked, she can see the etheric almost in its entirety, and we understand that she is now beginning to see the aura. She is one of the fortunate ones who can see Nature Spirits and the aura of flowers. As an artist she has been able to paint flowers with the aura around them.

To show you that clairvoyant powers are not limited to any locality, but are universal to the world, we are going to quote a letter from a very talented lady in Yugoslavia. We wrote to this lady and told her that we would like to incorporate within this course something of her experience, and so she wrote us a letter giving us permission to quote from it. We have altered the English very slightly to make it easier for people to follow. Here it is:

"Dearest Friends in other parts of the world! We really live in a time which asks us day by day—to be or not to be. The time is over to sit like a cat behind the stove. The life as well as the eternity put before us the question Yes or No? What Yes or No do we mean? We mean shall we starve our souls and make our bodies ill, or feed our souls and make our bodies healthy, beautiful and in harmony. Why do I always speak about the soul, something we cannot see, what the surgeons cannot take out and present to us on a plate? Dearest Friends, if you believe in the existence of the soul or not, the soul is there! Have you a moment of time to spare please? Do not run to the movies nor to the football game nor go shopping or for a drive, listen for a moment, for this is a very important matter indeed.

"In the Western part of our Earth we have not very many people who can see the so-called invisible world, who can see the auras of people. That means the light or the shadow, if there is a light or a very earthbound soul around the body, and especially around the head of a person. The soul is the eternal, undisturbable part of us, it is our Higher Body and without it we could not exist. I had the gift to see auras from my earliest days.

"When I was a little child I thought that all people could see what I could see. Later, when they called me a liar or declared me insane, I understood that other people could not see what I saw. Let me point out the way that I follow.

"Have you ever noticed the lines around the wood in the inner part of a tree? It indicates the years during which the tree has lived, you can tell of the lean years and of the fruitful years. Nothing at all remains without signs. Nothing. I once stood before an old church and saw what other people could not see on the Earth. Around the building was a wonderful light, around this light following the form of the building were fine lines as in the wood. I looked over the lines and told the people about them. It was a line for every century exactly, it was at the old church of Remete near Zagreb, the capital of Croatia. From that time I was able to tell the lines around old buildings and to say how old they were. Once a friend asked me, 'How old is this chapel?' 'I see nothing,' I answered, 'Not a line around yet, only a light.' 'All right,' she said, 'This chapel is not a hundred years old yet.'

"You see, if a building has its 'soul' how much more has something living. I can see the aura of the wood, of the trees and the meadows, the flowers, and especially after sunset. This mild but intense light is around all living creatures, around your dog as well as around your cat.

"Do you see the little bird there singing its evening song? How sprays of light are around the little bird, its soul flickering with happiness. But also, that little bird, a boy came and shot it down. The little aura flickered still a moment, and then vanished. It was like a cry through nature. I saw it, I felt it, and I talked about it, and they called me a fool.

"When I was 18 years of age, I stood before a mirror one day. It was nightfall and I was preparing to go to bed. The room was nearly dark, I was in a long white nightgown. All at once I saw a light in the mirror. It attracted me, I looked up and saw around me a blue and then a golden flame. Not knowing about the aura, I was frightened and I ran down to my parents screaming, 'I am burning.' It hurt me not at all, but what was it? They gasped at me, and then turned the light on during which time they saw nothing. But they turned the light off, and then they saw me as in living golden flames. Our servant came in and screamed with fright. She turned and ran away. I remembered then what I had seen on other beings, but it was rather different when I saw it on myself. Now I was really frightened. My father turned the light off and on, and off and on, and it was always the same—when the light was off I glowed with the golden light, when the room light was on, my glow could not be so clearly seen.

"I found all this interesting when I felt sure that I was not being harmed at all, and from then on I took very great interest in looking at the auras of other people.

"Do you know what fear means? In war I often was very frightened seeing the aura of my fellowmen when the bombers went over us and the bombs fell down. Once when I was in a prison under the Nazi regime I was in a cellar, condemned to death. I was taken to the torture chamber because I had certain information which my keepers wanted. I saw the aura of other people who were being tortured, it was terrible, so narrow round the body, so poor and without real light, nearly vanishing, nearly dying away, and worse still, when I heard the cries of agony when people were dying of torture, the aura itself flickered. Something rose in me, however, something of a holy force. Was there not written in the Holy Scriptures, 'Fear only those who kill the soul, but not those who kill the body?' I began to concentrate, and to try and cheer up the others, I felt my aura spread out again, I saw the aura of the others becoming healthier. Another woman helped me in this task, and at last the cell containing those condemned to death began to be more cheerful, we all began to sing. I came through all the questionings and all the long hours, and all the pain, unharmed because I concentrated on eternity, I concentrated on the Real Life after this awful dream. The torturers could do nothing with me, and at last, angry, they threw me out of the prison because I was demoralizing them!

"If I had given way to fright, to terror, I and my sixteen comrades—victims of persecution—would have been killed.

"We of the West, we Europeans, have much to learn from the Far East. We have to learn to conquer our imaginations and to overcome fear.

"As I see it, the aura of Western people flickers a lot, they are never quiet, seldom in harmony, and our disorderly aura infects other auras and becomes like an epidemic. Hitler would not have succeeded with his ranting speeches unless the aura of people became afflicted, and influenced by the aura of Hitler. Hitler could only succeed because his listeners could not control their own imagination.

"Are you tired? Will you read a little longer? Let us go to the poorest of men, to the lunatics, let us go to a mental home in Zagreb. Many days ago I made studies through the iron wire there looking at the auras. But they were not the worst cases: A friend of mine introduced me to the senior physician, a very skeptical man. I told him that I wished to observe the auras of his patients. He looked at me as being worthy of incarceration as a lunatic, then at last he decided that he would let me see some of them. At last attendants brought in a very sick woman indeed, she was a terrible looking woman, her eyes rolled and her teeth ground together, and hair stood out like devilish flames around her head. It really was a fearful sight. But it was nothing to what I saw in the invisible world. I saw the soul of the woman right out of her body in a wild struggle with the dark shadow who tried to get possession of the body. All around was in a whirl, and in disharmony. Eventually the woman was taken away, and I told the doctor that that woman could not be cured because she was indeed the victim of demoniac possession!"

So we will bring this particular lesson to a close with the remarks about what this very talented lady of Yugoslavia has seen. You also can see with practice, with perseverance, and with faith. Remember, Rome was not built in a day, and a doctor or a lawyer is not made overnight, they have to study to succeed, and so have you; there is no easy, no painless way out!

Lesson Nineteen

WE HAVE FROM time to time mentioned the Akashic Record. Now let us discuss this most fascinating subject, for the Akashic Record is something which concerns every person and every creature who has ever lived. With the Akashic Record we can travel back along history, we can see all that has happened, not merely upon this world but upon other worlds also, for the scientist is now coming to realize what occultists have always known, that other worlds are occupied by other persons not necessarily human, but sentient beings, nonetheless.

Before we can say much about the Akashic Record, we have to know something about the nature of energy or matter. Matter, we are told, is indestructible, it goes on forever. Waves, electric waves, are indestructible. Scientists have recently found that if a current is induced in a coil of copper wire, the temperature of which is reduced to as near absolute zero as possible, the induced current carries on and on and on, and never grows less. We all know that at normal temperatures the current would soon diminish and die out because of various resistances. So, science has found a new medium; science has found that if a copper conductor be reduced sufficiently in temperature a current continues to flow and remain the same without any outside source of energy. In time scientists will discover that human beings have other senses, other abilities, but they will not be discovered yet for the scientist proceeds slowly and not always surely!

We said that waves are indestructible. Let us look at the behavior of light waves. Light reaches us from far distant stars in universes remote from our own. Great telescopes on this Earth are probing out into space, in other words, they are gathering light from vastly distant places. Some of the stars from which we receive light sent out that light long before this world, even this universe, came into existence. Light is a very fast thing indeed, the speed of light is so fast that we can hardly imagine it but that is because we are in human bodies and are greatly bogged down with all sorts of physical limitations. What we consider to be "fast" here has a different meaning in a different plane of existence. By way of illustration, let us say that a round of existence for a human is seventy-two thousand years. During that round, a person comes again and again to different worlds, to different bodies. The seventy-two thousand years, then, is the length of our "school term."

When we refer to "light" instead of radio or electric waves or other waves, we do so merely because light can be observed without any equipment, a radio wave cannot. We can see the light of the Sun, the light of the Moon, and if we have a good telescope or a powerful pair of binoculars we can see the light of the far distant stars which started out before Earth was even a cloud of hydrogen molecules floating in space.

Light is also used as a measure of time or distance. Astronomers refer to light years, and we are going to tell you again that light coming from a far distant world may still be traveling after that world has ceased to exist, from which it is clear that we may be getting a picture from something that is no longer there, something that died years ago. If you find that difficult to understand, look at it in this way; we have a star out in the remote vastnesses of space. For years, for centuries, that star has been reflecting light waves down to Earth. The light waves may take a thousand, ten thousand, or a million years to reach Earth, because a star, the source of the light, is so very distant. One day the star is in collision with another star, there may be a great flash of light or there may be extinction. For our purpose let us say that there is total extinction. So the light is gone, but for a thousand, or ten thousand, or a million years after the light is gone, light still reaches us because it takes all that time to cover the distance between the original source of light and ourselves. Thus, we should be seeing light after its source ceases to exist.

Let us assume something that is utterly impossible while we are in the physical body, but which is quite easy and commonplace when out of the body. Let us assume that we can travel faster than thought. We need to travel faster than thought because thought has a very definite speed as any doctor can tell you. It is actually known how quickly a person reacts to any given situation, how quickly or how slowly a person can put on the brakes of a car, or move the wheel to swerve aside. It is known how quickly thought impulses travel from head to toe. We, for the purpose of this discussion, want to travel instantly. Let us imagine that we can go instantly to a planet which is receiving light which was emitted from the Earth three thousand years ago. So we upon this distant planet will be receiving light sent from the Earth three thousand years ago. Supposing we have a telescope of a quite unimagined type with which we can see the surface of the Earth, or interpret the rays of light reaching us, then this light sent out three thousand years ago would show us scenes of the world enacted at that time. We should see life as it was in ancient Egypt, we would see the barbarous Western world where people ran about covered in skins or less, and in China we should find quite a high civilization, so much different from what is there at the present time!

If we could instantly travel closer, we should see quite different pictures. Let us move to a planet which is so distant from the Earth that light takes a thousand years for it to travel between that planet and Earth. Then we should see scenes of Earth as they were enacted a thousand years ago, we should see a high civilization in India, we should see the spread of Christianity throughout the Western world, and perhaps some of the invasions of South America. The world would also look somewhat different from its present appearance because all the time a coast line is altering, and is rising from the sea, shores are being eroded. In a lifetime not much difference is noted, but a thousand years would give us chance to see and appreciate the difference.

At present we are upon a world which has most remarkable limitations, we are able to perceive and to receive impressions on only a very limited range of frequencies. If we could see some of our out of the body abilities to the full as we can in the astral world, we should see things in a very different light, we should perceive that all matter is indeed indestructible, every experience that ever has been in the world is still radiating outward in the form of waves. With special abilities we could intercept those waves in much the same way as we can intercept waves of light. Take as a simple example of this an ordinary slide projector; you switch on your slide projector in a darkened room and you put a slide in the appropriate place. If you put a screen—a white screen for preference—in front of the lens of the projector at a certain distance from it, and you focus the light on the screen, you see a picture. But if you have your projector projecting its picture out the window and into the darkness beyond, you see just a faint beam of light with no picture. It follows that the light must be intercepted, must be reflecting on something before it can be fully perceived and appreciated. Take a searchlight on a clear and cloudless night; you might see a faint tracery of light, but only when the searchlight impinges on a cloud or an airplane do you actually see it as it is.

It has long been the dream of humanity to have a thing called "time travel." This, obviously, is a fantastic conception while one is in the flesh and upon the Earth, because here in the flesh we are sadly limited, our bodies are most imperfect instruments, and as we are here to learn we have implanted in us much doubt, much indecision, and before we can be convinced, we want proof—the ability to pull a thing to pieces to see how it works and to make sure it does not work again. When we get beyond the Earth and into the astral, or even beyond the astral, time travel is as simple as a visit to the movie theater.

The Akashic Record, then, is a form of vibration, not necessarily light vibrations because it also embraces sound. It is a form of vibration which upon Earth has no term that can describe it. The nearest one can do is to liken it to a radio wave. We have about us at all times radio waves coming in from all parts of the world; every one of them brings in a different program, different languages, different music, different times. It is possible that waves are coming in from one part of the world which contains a program which, to us, is being broadcast tomorrow. All these waves are coming to us constantly, but we are oblivious to them, and not until we have some mechanical device which we call a radio set can we receive those waves and slow them down so they become

audible and comprehensible to us. Here, with a mechanical
or electrical device, we slow down radio frequency waves
and convert them to audio frequency waves. In much the
same way, if, on Earth, we could slow down the waves of
the Akashic Record we should undoubtedly be able to put
authentic historical scenes on the television screen, and then
the historians would throw a fit when they saw that the history
as printed in books is completely, completely wrong!

The Akashic Record is the indestructible vibrations consisting of the sum total of human knowledge that emanates
from the world in much the same way as the radio program
is broadcast, it goes on and on. Everything that has happened
on this Earth still exists in vibration form. When we get out
of the body we do not use a special device to understand
these waves; we use nothing to slow them down, instead, in
getting out of the body, our own "wave receptors" are speeded
up so that, with practice, with training, we can receive that
which we term the Akashic Record.

Let us get back to this problem of outstripping light. It
will be easier if we forget about light for the moment, and
deal instead with sound, because sound is slower and we do
not have to have such vast distances before getting results.
Supposing you are standing out in the open and you suddenly
hear a very fast moving jet plane. You hear the sound, but it
is useless to look up to that point from whence the sound
appears to be coming because the jet plane is going faster
than the sound, and so will be ahead of the sound itself. In
World War II great bombs were sent from enslaved Europe
to cause destruction in England. The bombs crashed down on
houses, wrecking them and killing people. The first warning
that people had that these bombs were about was the noise
of the explosion and the crashing of falling stones, and the
screams of the injured. Later, when the dust was subsiding
somewhat, came the sound of the bomb arriving! This quite
weird experience was caused by the fact that the bomb trav-

eled so very much faster than the sound it made. Hence it was that the bomb did all its destruction before its sound arrived.

One can stand on a hilltop and look at a gun placed perhaps upon another hilltop. One cannot hear the shell from the gun when it is exactly overhead, but the sound comes shortly after when the shell is still speeding off into the distance. No person has ever been killed by a shell which he heard, for the shell arrives first and the sound later. That is why it is so amusing when people in wars used to duck at the sound of a shell passing overhead. Actually, if they could hear the sound it meant that the shell had passed by. Sound is slow compared to sight or light. Standing again upon this hilltop, we can look at a gun being fired, we can see the flash from the muzzle, and much later—the time depending upon the distance we are from the gun—we hear the sound of the shell passing overhead. You might have watched a man chopping a tree; the man would be some distance away, you would actually see the axe hitting the tree trunk, and then a short time after you would hear the "thunk-thunk" of the sound. This is an experience which most of us have had.

The Akashic Record contains the knowledge of everything that has happened on this world. Worlds elsewhere have their own Akashic Records in much the same way as countries outside our own have their own radio programs. Those who know how can tune into the Akashic Record of any world, not merely of one's own, and one can then see events of history, one can see how the history books have been falsified. But there is more to the Akashic Record than just satisfying idle curiosity—one can look into this record and see what went wrong with one's own plans. When we die to the Earth we go to another plane of existence where every single one of us has to face up to what we did, or what we did not do; we see the whole of our past life with the speed of thought, we see it through the Akashic Record, see it not just from the time that we were born but from the time that we planned how and where we would be born. Then, having that knowledge, having seen our errors, we plan again and try once more just like a child at school seeing what went wrong with answers to the examination papers, and taking the examination all over again.

Naturally enough, it takes a long, long training before one can see the Akashic Record, but with training, with practice and faith it can be done and is indeed being done constantly. Do you think, maybe, we should pause a moment and discuss this thing called "faith?"

Faith is a definite thing which can and must be cultivated in much the same way as a habit or a greenhouse plant must be cultivated. Faith is not as hardy as a weed, it is indeed more like a greenhouse plant. It must be pampered, must be fed, must be looked after. To obtain faith we must repeat, and repeat, and repeat our affirmation of faith so that the knowledge of it is driven into our subconscious. This subconscious is nine-tenths of us, that is, by far the greater part of us.

We often liken it unto a lazy old man who just does not want to be disturbed. The old man is reading his newspapers, perhaps he has his pipe in his mouth and his feet are encased in comfortable slippers. He is really tired of all the racket, all the noise, all the distraction constantly going on around him. Through years of experience, he has learned to shield himself from all except the most insistent interruptions and distractions. Like an old man who is partly deaf, he doesn't hear when he is called the first time. The second time he is called he doesn't hear because he doesn't want to hear, because he thinks it might be work for him, or some interruption of his lazy leisure. The third time he starts to get irritable because the caller is disturbing his trend of thoughts while he is perhaps more anxious to read the racing results than to do anything which requires effort.

Keep on and on repeating your faith and then the "old man" will come to life with a jerk, and when the knowledge is implanted in your subconscious then you will have automatic faith. We must make it clear here that faith is not belief; you can say, "I believe that tomorrow is Monday," and that means a certain thing. You would not say, "I have faith that tomorrow is Monday", because that would mean a completely different thing. Faith is something which usually grows up with us. We become a Christian, or a Buddhist, or a Jew because, usually, our parents were Christians, Buddhists, or Jews. We have faith in our parents—we believe that what our parents believed was correct—and so our "faith" became the same as our parents'. Certain things which cannot definitely be proved while upon the Earth require faith, other things which can be proved can be believed or disbelieved. There is a distinction, and one should become aware of that distinction.

But, first of all, what do you want to believe, what is it that requires your faith? Decide what it is that needs faith, think of it from all angles. Is it faith in a religion, faith in an ability? Think of it from as many angles as you can, and then, making sure that you think of it in a positive way, affirm—state—to yourself that you can do this or that, or that you will do this or that, or that you firmly believe in this or that. You must keep on affirming it. Unless you do so affirm you will never have faith. Great religions have faithful followers. Those faithful followers are ones who have been to church, or chapel, or synagogue, or temple, and by repeated prayers, not merely on their own behalf but by others also, their subconscious has become aware that there are some things which must be "a faith."

In the Far East there are such things as mantras. A person will say a certain thing—a mantra—and say it again and again, and repeat it time after time. Possibly the person will not even know what the mantra is about! That does not matter because the founders of the religion who composed the mantra will have arranged it in such a way that the vibrations engendered in repeating the mantra knock into the subconscious the thing

desired. Soon, even though the person does not fully understand the mantra, it becomes part of the person's subconscious, and the faith then is purely automatic. In much the
same way, if you repeat prayers time after time, you begin to
believe them. It is all a matter of getting your subconscious
to understand and to cooperate, and once you have faith then
you do not have to bother any more because your subconscious will always remind you that you have this faith, and
that you can do those certain things.

Repeat to yourself time after time that you are gong to
see an aura, that you are going to be telepathic, that you are
going to do this or that, whatever it is that you particularly
want to do. Then in time you will do this. All successful people,
all those who become millionaires or inventors are people
who have faith in themselves, they have faith that they can do
what they set out to do, because believing in themselves
first, believing in their own powers and abilities, they then
generated the faith which made that belief come true. If you
keep on telling yourself that you are going to succeed, you
will succeed, but you will only succeed if you keep on with
your affirmation of success and not let doubt (the negative of
faith) intrude. Try this affirmation of success, and the results
will truly astonish you.

You may have heard of people who can tell another
person what they were in a past life, what they were doing.
That comes from the Akashic Record, for many people in their
sleep travel into the astral and see the Akashic Record.When
they return in the morning, as we have already discussed, they
may bring back a distorted memory, so while some of the
things they say are true, others are distortions. You will find
that most of the things you hear about relate to suffering.
People seem to have been torturers, seem to have been all
sorts of things—mainly bad. That is because we come to this
Earth as to a school, we have to remember at all times that
people have to have hardship to purge them of their faults, in

much the same way that ore is placed in a furnace and sub-jected to intense heat so that the dross or wastage rises to the surface where it can be skimmed off and discarded. Humans have to undergo stresses which drive them almost, but not quite, to the breaking point so that their spirituality may be tested, and their faults may be eradicated. People come to this Earth to learn things, and people learn much more quickly and more permanently by hardship than by kindness.

This is a world of hardship, it is a training school which is almost a reformatory, and although there are rare kindnesses which shine out like the beam of a beacon light on a dark night, much of the world is strife. Look at the history of nations if you dispute this, look at all the incipient wars. It is indeed a world of impurity, and it makes it difficult for Higher Entities to come here as they must in order to supervise what is going on. It is a fact that a Higher Entity coming to this Earth must take up some impurity which will act almost as an anchor, and keep them in contact with the Earth. The High Entity who comes here cannot come in his own pure, unsullied form, because he could not stand the sorrows and the trials of the Earth. So, be careful when you think that such-and-such a person cannot be so high as some people say because he is too fond of this or too fond of that. As long as he does not drink, then he might be quite high. Drink, though, cancels out all high abilities.

Many of the greatest clairvoyants and telepaths have some physical affliction because suffering can often increase the rate of vibration and confer telepathy or clairvoyance upon the sufferer. You cannot know of a person's spirituality by just looking at him. Do not judge a person to be an evil person because he is sick; the sickness may have been taken on deliberately in order that the person can increase his or her rate of vibration for a special task. Do not judge a person harshly because he or she uses a swear word, or does not altogether act as you think that a Great Person should act. It may indeed be a Great Person who is using swear words or some other vice in order to have an anchor to enable him or her to remain upon the Earth again, provided that the person does not engage in drink, the person may quite definitely be the Higher Entity which you originally thought him to be.

There is much impurity on Earth, and all that is impure decays; only the pure and the incorruptible lives on. That is one of the reasons why we come to Earth; in the spirit world beyond the astral you cannot have corruption, you cannot have evil on the higher planes, so people come to Earth to learn the hard way. And again, and again, a Great Entity coming to Earth will take a vice or an affliction, knowing that as he or she came for a special task, that affliction or vice will not be held as karma (we shall deal with that later) but instead be regarded as a tool, as an anchor, which passes away as corruption along with the physical body.

There is a further point which we are going to make, and it is this; great reformers in this life are sometimes those who in a previous life were great offenders in the line in which he or she now reforms. Hitler, undoubtedly, will come back as a great reformer. Many of the people from the Spanish Inquisition have come back as great reformers. It is a thought worth thinking of. Remember—the middle way is the way in which to live. Do not be so bad that you have to suffer for it later, and if you are so pure, so holy, that everyone is beneath you, then you cannot stay on this Earth. Fortunately, however, no one is *that* pure!

Lesson Twenty

SOON WE HOPE to deal with telepathy, clairvoyance, and psychometry, but first of all you must permit us a digression—permit us to deal with another subject. We are quite aware that you are thinking by now that we wander off the subject, but that is deliberate; we know what we have in mind, and often it pays for us to draw your attention to a subject and then go on to something else which is so very necessary by way of a foundation.

We will make it clear now that people who want to be clairvoyant, who want to be telepathic and to have psychometric abilities will have to proceed slowly. You cannot force development beyond a certain limit. If you will consider the world of nature you will find that exotic orchids are indeed greenhouse plants, and if they have been forced in their development, then they are very fragile blooms indeed. The same applies to everything the growth of which has to be stimulated artificially, or which has its growth forced. Greenhouse plants are not hardy, they are not reliable, they fall prey to all sorts of remarkable ailments. We want you to have a very healthy dose of telepathy, we want you to able to see into the past by clairvoyance, and we want you to be in such a position that you can pick up a stone, for instance, from the seashore and tell what has happened to that stone throughout the years. It is possible, you know, for a really good psychometrist to pick up an article on the seashore where it has not been touched by a human being, and to visualize quite clearly the time when that fragment of stone was perhaps embodied in a mountain. This is not exaggeration, it is very ordinary, very easy—when one knows how! Let us, then, lay a good foundation, because one cannot build a house on shifting sands and expect the house to last for very long. In dealing with our foundation let us state first that inner composure and tranquility are two of the cornerstones of our foundation, for unless one has inner composure one will not have much success at telepathy or clairvoyance. Inner composure is a very definite must if one is going to progress beyond the most elementary primary stages.

Humans are indeed a mass of conflicting emotions. One looks about and finds people hurrying about in the street, dashing about in cars, or rushing off to catch a bus. Then there is the last minute dash to the shops to lay in supplies possibly before the shops close for the weekend. We are always in a jangled state; we seethe and boil, and our brains send off sparks of rage and frustration. Often we will find ourselves growing hot, we will find that we are under tension, that we have queer pressures within us. At such times we feel that we could explode. Yes, you might almost do that! But it will not help one at all in the field of esoteric research if one has such uncontrolled brain waves that one blanks out the incoming signals. The signals are coming in all the time from everywhere from everyone, and if we will open our minds we will pick up and comprehend those signals.

Have you ever tried to listen to radio during a thunderstorm? Have you ever tried to watch some television program while someone was parked just outside your window and you were getting the car ignition as zig-zag flashes through the screen? Perhaps you have attempted listening to a far distant station over the howl and crackle of static generated by an electric storm. It is not easy! Some of us are interested in shortwave reception and listen in to the whole world, listen to the news from different countries, listen to music from various continents. If you have done much in shortwave work, and have listened to far off places, you will know how very difficult it is at times to pick up speech because of all the interference caused by static, both manmade and natural. Car ignition noises, the clicking on and off of the thermostat, the refrigerator, or perhaps someone is playing about with the doorbell just when we want to listen. We get hotter and hotter under the collar as we try to concentrate and pick up the message from the radio. Until we can get clear of some of that "static" in our own minds, we are going to have difficulty with telepathy, for the noise a human brain churns out is far worse than even that from the most battered old car. You may think this is exaggeration, but as your powers increase in this direction you will find that we have rather understated the matter.

Let us develop this theme a little further because we must be quite sure of what we are doing before we do it, we must be quite sure of the obstacles in our path, because until we know the obstacles, we cannot overcome them. Let us consider it from a different angle; it is a fairly easy matter to telephone from one continent to another provided that there be a suitable cable laid beneath the ocean. The transatlantic telephone line from, let us say, England to New York, or to

Adelaide from England, is a case in point. Using these telephone lines under the water one still gets garbled patches of
speech. At times, there will also be fading, but on the whole
most people understand quite well what is being said from
one continent to the other. Unfortunately, parts of the world
are still not connected by modern technology. In certain
primitive areas, there were telephone "radio links." These
horrendous contraptions should never, never be dignified
by the name "telephone" because using them appeared to
be a feat of endurance. Speech was frequently garbled
beyond recognition, speech was chopped up, high and low
frequencies cut off. Instead of getting a human tone of voice
that we could comprehend we got a flat monotone which
could have been spewed out without inflection by some
robot. One strained and strained to make out what was
being said, but all the time there was a further grave
disadvantage; one had to keep talking all the time (even if
one had nothing to say) in order to "keep the circuit open."
Added to that there was the static which we have already
mentioned, as well as the various refractions and reflections
from the different ionized layers around the Earth. We
mention this to show that even with the best equipment
on Earth, speech by radio telephone was a matter of hit or
miss, and in our experience it is more often miss than hit.
We personally find telepathy to be far far easier to use than
a radio telephone!

You may wonder why we keep on writing about radio
and electronics and electricity. The answer is because the
brain and the body generate electricity. The brain and all the
muscles send out pulsing electrons which are, in fact, the
radio program of the human body. Much of the behavior of
the human body, and much of the phenomena of clairvoyance,
telepathy, psychometry, and all the rest of it can be so easily
understood by reference to the science of radio and electronics. We are trying to make this easy for you, so we are going

to ask you to very carefully consider all this matter about electronics and about radio; it does mean much to you if you study electronics.

The more you study radio and electronics, the more easily will you progress in your development. Delicate instruments need to be protected from shock. You would not expect to have an expensive television set and bang it about; you would not expect to have an expensive watch and keep banging it against the wall. We have the most expensive receivers of all—our brains—and if we are going to use that "receiver" to the best effect we must protect it from shock. If we are going to let ourselves become agitated or frustrated, then we are going to generate a type of wave within us which will inhibit reception of waves without. In telepathy we have to keep as calm as possible otherwise we are going to be wasting our time in making any attempt whatever at receiving the thoughts of others. The first time we shall not get much result in telepathy. So, let us concentrate on composure.

Whenever we think, we generate electricity. If we think calmly and without any strong emotion, then our brain electricity will follow a fairly smooth frequency without high peaks, and without low valleys. If we have a high peak it means that something is interrupting the even tenor of our thoughts. We must be sure that there are no excessive voltages generated, and nothing which could cause alarm and despondency must be permitted within our thinking processes.

We must at all times cultivate inner composure, cultivate a tranquil manner. No doubt it is annoying if you are hanging out the washing and the telephone rings when you just have your hands full of wet soggy clothes. No doubt it is frightfully irritating when you miss the special bargain for the week at the local store, but all these things are very mundane, they do not help us at all when we leave this world. When we do terminate our stay upon Earth it will not matter greatly, if at all, whether we have dealt with the great supermarkets or with the little man in the corner store. Let us repeat again (in case you haven't read it before) that we cannot take a single penny away with us to the next life, but we can and do take away all the knowledge that we have gained, for the distilled essence of all that we learn upon Earth is that which makes us what we are going to be in the next life. Therefore let us concentrate on knowledge, on the things which we can take away. At present the world has gone money-mad, possession-mad. Countries such as Canada and the United States of America are living under a false standard of prosperity, everyone seems to be in debt, everyone is borrowing from the finance companies (alias the old fashioned moneylender, now done up with chromium plate). People want new cars, each one flashier than the one of the year before. People dash about, they have no time for the serious things of life, they are chasing the things that do not matter. The only things that matter are the things we learn; we take away with us all the knowledge that we acquire during our stay on Earth, we leave behind us—if we have any—money and possessions for someone else to squander. Wherefore it behooves us to concentrate on the things which will be truly ours—knowledge.

One of the easiest ways of acquiring tranquility is by breathing in a regular pattern. Most people, unfortunately, breathe in a manner which could be termed "suck-blow, suck-blow," they pant along really starving the brain of oxygen. People seem to think that air is rationed, they have to gulp it in and puff it out. They seem to think the air they take in is hot, or something, for no sooner is it in than they are anxious to get rid of it and get the next load.

We should learn to breathe slowly and deeply. We should make sure that all the stale air is removed from our lungs. If we breathe with only the top of our lungs, that air which is at the bottom becomes more and more stale. The better our air supply is, the better our brain power will be, for we cannot live without oxygen and the brain is the first thing to be starved of oxygen. If the brain is deprived of the minimum amount of oxygen we feel tired—sleepy—we become slow in our motion, and we find it difficult to think. Sometimes, too, we find that we get a bad headache, then we go out into the fresh air which cures the headache, and also proves that one does need plenty of oxygen.

A regular breathing pattern soothes ruffled emotions. If you are feeling thoroughly bad tempered—"out of sorts"—and really would like to do violence to someone, take a deep breath instead, the deepest breath you can manage, and hold it for a few seconds. Then let it out slowly over a few seconds. Do that a few times, and you will find that you calm down more quickly than you thought possible.

Do not just suck in breath as fast as you can, and then blow it out as fast as you can. Draw in the breath slowly, steadily, and think—as is truly the case—that you are inhaling life and vitality itself. Let us give an illustration; compress your chest, and try to expel as much air as you possibly can, force your lungs in so that—if you wish—your tongue is hanging out from the lack of air. Then, over some ten seconds of time, completely fill your lungs, throw out your chest, take in as much air as you can, and then cram in a little more. When you have got in as much air as you possibly can, hold it for five seconds, and after that five seconds slowly let out the air, so slowly that you take seven seconds to get rid of the air within you. Exhale completely, force your muscles inward to squeeze out as much air as you can. Then start all over again. It might be a good idea if you do this half a dozen times, and you will find that your frustrations and your bad mood has gone, you will feel better inside too; you will find that you are beginning to get inner composure.

If you are going for an interview which really matters, before you actually go into the interview room, take some deep breaths. You will find that your racing pulse will race no more, it will steady down, you will find that you are more confident, have less to worry about, and if you do this, your interviewer will be impressed with your obvious appearance of confidence. Try it!

There are a shocking number of frustrations and irritations in everyday life, and these things are very harmful indeed. Civilization is quite the opposite of that. The more one gets tied up with the trammels of civilization, the more difficult it is to get peace. The man or woman in the heart of a great city is often more irritable, more nervous, than the man or woman in the heart of the countryside. So it becomes more and more necessary to gain some control over emotions. People who are frustrated and irritable find that their gastric juices become more and more concentrated. These juices are, of course, acids, and as they become more and more concentrated they boil up within us, and eventually reach such a degree of concentration that the inner protective lining of our stomach or other organs cannot resist the attack of the strong acid. Possibly some part of our inner lining is thinner than the rest. Possibly we have some small blemish inside, some hard piece of food which we have swallowed may have caused slight irritation in the stomach. Then the acid has a place at which it can work. It works and works on that thinner place, or irritated spot, and in time it penetrates the protective layer within us. The result is a gastric ulcer which leads us to considerable despondency and pain. As you have probably heard, gastric ulcers are known as the complaint of the irritable and nervous. Let us think about all these irritations; you may be wondering where to get the money to pay the gas bill, or why the electric meter man is fussing around your door when you are busy with something else. You may wonder why do so many silly people send you stupid circulars through the mail? Why should you throw them away? Why not let the sender destroy them first and save you the trouble? Well—take it easy—think to yourself, ask yourself this question, "Will all this matter in fifty or a hundred years time?" Whenever you get frustrated, whenever you get almost overcome with the press of ordinary, everyday living, whenever you think that you are going to be submerged in your troubles and your difficulties, think about it again, think—"Will any of these matters, any of these worries, be important in fifty or a hundred years time?"

This age of civilization, so-called, is a very trying age indeed. Everything conspires to make us build up unnatural brain waves, conspires to make strange voltages generate within our brain cells. Normally when one thinks there is a fairly rhythmical pattern of brain waves that doctors can chart with special instruments. If the brain waves follow a certain pattern, then we are stated to have some mental affliction, so that when a person has a mental sickness probably the first thing that is done is to chart the brain waves to see how they diverge from the normal. It is a fact known to Easterners that if a person can subdue the abnormal brain waves, then sanity returns. In the Far East there are various methods used by medical priests whereby the distressed person—the person who has a mental affliction—can be assisted in restoring his brain waves to normalcy.

Women, particularly at the change of life, are subject to the generation of a different wave form within the brain. This, of course, is because at the change of life various secretions are shut off or diverted to other channels, and usually the woman in question has been listening to so many "old wives' tales" that she really does think she is going to be in for a bad time, and because she firmly believes she is going to have difficulties she does. There is no need for any difficulties at the change of life provided a person is properly prepared. The more unfortunate cases are those women who have had an operation termed hysterectomy. Hysterectomy is an operation whereby the menopause is brought on forcibly by surgical means. Admittedly that is a secondary reason, the operation is usually for some specific purpose like disease, but the end result is the same; a woman has an operation—hysterectomy—and the sudden termination of the former way of living and the sudden diversion of essential hormones, etc., causes a severe electrical storm in the brain which, for a time, may make the woman even unstable. Suitable treatment and sympathetic understanding really can cure such an unfortunate sufferer. We mention this merely to indicate that the body is an electric generator, and it is so very essential to keep that generator with a constant output, because if we have constant output we may be said to have composure and tranquility, but if the output is upset and varies through worry or certain operations, then tranquility is temporarily lost. But it can definitely be regained!

Let us get back, though, to our "fifty or a hundred years time." If you do good to a person, then that is something that will matter in fifty to a hundred years time, because if you do good, you brighten some person's outlook, just as if you do harm to a person then you depress their outlook. The more good you can do to others, the more you can gain yourself. It is an esoteric law that you cannot receive until you are willing to give first. If you give, be it service or money or love, then you in your turn will get service or money or love, and no matter what you give, no matter what you receive, everything has to be paid for in time. If you receive a kindness you have to give a kindness, but that is not to be dealt with in this lesson as we will refer to it in more detail when we deal with karma.

Be sure to keep yourself calm, be sure to let yourself become tranquil, let yourself realize that all these petty restrictions, all these asinine interruptions when we are trying to think or trying to do something will not matter in a few years time; they are pinpricks, petty irritations, and they should be relegated to their correct status as annoyances and nothing more. Inner composure, peace and tranquility are there for you if you will accept them. All you have to do is to breathe so that your brain gets the maximum oxygen and think that all these silly little irritations will not matter in half a century's time. Then you will see how unimportant they are.

Do you see what we are getting at? We are trying to show you that most of the great worries simply do not happen. We have something threatening us, we fear that something unpleasant is about to occur, we work ourselves up into a frenzy of fright, and we go about in such a state that we hardly know if we are on our heads or our feet. But soon we find that our fears were unjustified, nothing happened! All the fright was for nothing. We have got a real mixture of adrenalin within us all boiled up ready to galvanize us into action, and then when the fright passes the adrenalin has to be dissipated and it makes us feel quite weak, we might even shake with the reaction. Many of the world's famous people have said that their major worries never happened, but that they still worried and then found that they had been wasting time. If you are troubled, you are not tranquil. If you are agitated, you cannot have inner composure, and instead of being able to receive a telepathic message, you are radiating—broadcasting—a dire message of utter chaos, of frustration which not merely blanks out your own reception of telepathic messages, but blanks out reception quite a distance around you. So, for your own sake, and for the sake of others, practice equanimity, keep calm, remember again that all these minor irritations are minor irritations and nothing more. They are sent to try you, and they certainly do!

Practice composure, practice seeing your difficulties in the correct perspective. It may be annoying to find that you cannot go to the movies tonight, particularly as it may be the last night that film is shown, but it is not of earth-shaking importance after all. It is of importance that you learn, how you progress, because the more you learn now the more you take away with you to the next life, and the more learning you take away to the next life, the less the number of times you have to come back to this doleful old world of ours.

We suggest that you lie down, let yourself relax. Lie down and shuffle about a bit so that no muscle, no part of you is under tension. Lightly clasp your hands together and breathe deeply and regularly. As you breathe, think in rhythm with the breathing, "peace-peace-peace." If you will practice that, you will find that a truly divine sense of peace and tranquility will steal over you. Once again, push out any intruding thoughts of discord, concentrating your thoughts upon peace, upon quietness and upon ease. If you think peace, you will have peace. If you think ease, you will have ease. We will say to you by way of concluding this lesson that if people would devote ten minutes out of every twenty-four hours to this, the doctors would go bankrupt for they would not have nearly so much illness to deal with!

Lesson Twenty-One

WE NOW COME IN this lesson to subjects which interest all of us—telepathy. You may have wondered why we have been stressing so much the similarity between human brain waves and radio waves. In this lesson you may get more enlightenment on that subject! Look at figure 9 on page 188. As you will see, we call it "the tranquil head." It is called "tranquil" because we must be in that state before we can do telepathy or clairvoyance or psychometry, that is why in our last lesson we dealt (did you say "ad nauseum"!) with those matters. We must be at ease within ourselves if we are going to progress.

Look at it this way; would you expect to get a good symphony concert if you were in the vicinity of a boiler factory? Would you be able to enjoy classical music—or whatever form of music you favor—if people were hopping up and

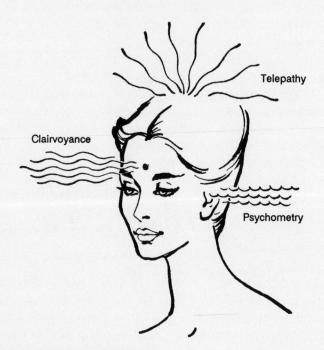

Figure 9. The tranquil head.

down around you screeching at the top of their voices? No,
you would either switch off the radio and run screaming
yourself, or you would tell everybody to be quiet! From fig. 9
you will see that there are different receptor areas of the brain.
The area which corresponds roughly to the halo picks up
telepathic waves. We will deal with the other waves later, first
we are dealing with telepathy. When we are tranquil, we can
pick up all sorts of impressions. They are merely the radio
waves of other people coming in and being absorbed by our
own receptive brains. You will agree that most people have
hunches. Most people at some time or other have had a most
strange impression that something was going to happen, or

that they should take some specific course of action. People who know no better call it a hunch. Actually it is merely unconscious, or subconscious, telepathy, that is, the person with the hunch was picking up a telepathic message sent out consciously or unconsciously by another person.

Intuition is the same type of thing; it is stated that women possess more intuition than men. The female brain is said to be smaller than that of the male, but of course that does not matter in the slightest. A lot of rubbish has been written about the size of brains affecting the size of intelligence. On the same basis, we suppose, an elephant should be a genius compared to human standards! The female brain can "resonate" in harmony with incoming messages, and, again in radio terms, the female brain is a radio set which can be tuned in to a station more easily than can the male brain. It is a matter of simplicity if you prefer that explanation. Do you remember the old old radio set that your father or your grandfather had? There were knobs and dials all over the place, and it was almost a feat of engineering to tune in the local station. One had to turn up filament controls to make sure that the tubes were at the right voltage. One had to tune in with a pair of slow motion knobs, often one had to move coils as well, and then there was the volume control. Your grandfather will tell you all about the first radios. Now—well, now one gets hold of a pocket radio, switches it on, moves a knob perhaps with one finger, and there is the program maybe from half way across the world. The female brain is like that, it is easier to tune than is the male brain.

We would also remind you of identical twins. It is an established fact that identical twins are nearly always in contact with each other, no matter how far they may be apart physically. You can have one twin in North America and another twin in South America, and you will get reports of happenings occurring to the pair of them simultaneously, you will get reports that each knows what the other is doing. That is because these two came from a single cell, came from a single egg, and so their brains are like a pair of carefully matched radio receivers or transmitters. They are "in tune" without any effort at all on the part of the owners.

Now you will want to know how you can do telepathy, for you can do it with practice and with faith, but no matter how much practice, no matter how much faith, you will not do it unless you have our old friend inner composure. The best way to practice is:—

Tell yourself for a day or two that on such-and-such a day at such-and-such a time you are going to make your brain receptive so that you can pick up, first general impressions, and then definite telepathic messages. Keep repeating to yourself, keep affirming to yourself, that you are going to succeed in this.

On the predetermined day, preferably in the evening, retire to a private room. Make sure that the lights are low, and that the temperature is just comfortable for you. Then recline in the position which you have found to be the most comfortable. Have in your hand a photograph of the person to whom you are most attached. Any light should be behind you so that it shines on or illuminates the photograph. Breathe deeply for a few minutes, and then clear your mind of all extraneous thoughts, think of the person whose photograph is in your hands, look at the photograph, visualize the person standing in front of you. What would this person say to you? What would you reply? Frame your thoughts. You can, if you like, say, "Speak to me—Speak to me." Then wait for a reply. If you are composed, if you have faith, you will get some stirring inside your brain. First you will be inclined to put it down to imagination, but it is not imagination but reality. If you dismiss it as idle imagination you will dismiss telepathy.

The easiest way of acquiring telepathic ability is to work with a person whom you know very well, and with whom you are on the most intimate terms of friendship. Both of you should discuss what you are going to do, you should both agree that on such-and-such a date at such-and-such a time you will get in touch with each other telepathically. Both of you should retire to rooms, it does not matter how far apart, it can even be a continent apart, for distance is no object. But you must make sure that you make allowance for any difference in time, for example—Buenos Aires may be two hours ahead of New York in time. You have to allow for that otherwise your experiment will fail. You also have to agree who is going to transmit and who is going to receive. You can do it easily if you synchronize your watches, and go by Greenwich mean time which will obviate any possibility of confusion. One can obtain Greenwich mean time almost anywhere, and if you decide to transmit first, and then after ten minutes, neither more nor less, but a definite fixed interval of time, your friend will transmit back. The first two or three times you will not necessarily succeed, but practice makes perfect. Remember that a baby cannot walk at the first attempt, the baby had to practice and fall down and crawl. You will not succeed necessarily at the first attempt at telepathy, but again practice makes perfect.

When you can send a telepathic message to a friend, or receive one, then you are well on the way to getting the thoughts of others, but you can only get their thoughts provided that you have no evil intent toward them. We are going to make one of our famous digressions here.

You can never, never, never use telepathy or clairvoyance or psychometry to do harm to another person, nor can any other person do harm to you by these means. It has often been stated that if an evil person were telepathic or clairvoyant he or she would be able to blackmail people who had made some slight mistake, but that emphatically is not the case; it is impossible. You cannot have light and darkness at the same time in the same place, and you cannot use telepathy for evil, that is an absolutely inexorable law of metaphysics. So—do not be alarmed, people do not read your thoughts to do you harm. No doubt many would like to, but they cannot do so. We mention that because of the fear that so many people have that a person by telepathy can know all the most secret fears and phobias. It is true that the purest minded people could pick up your thoughts, could see from your aura what your weak points were, but the pure person would not for one moment contemplate doing such a thing, and the impure person permanently lacks the ability.

We suggest that you practice telepathy with a friend, or if you cannot get a friend to cooperate, relax as we have said and let thoughts come in to you. You will find first that your head is a buzz of conflicting thoughts; it is similar to when you go into a crowd of people. There is a babble of conversation, just a horrible noise, everyone seems to be talking at the same time at the top of their voices. But if you try, you can single out one voice. You can do that also in telepathy. Practice, you must practice and have faith, and then, provided you keep calm about it all and have no intention of hurting any other person, you will be able to do telepathy.

From figure 9 on page 188, you will see that the rays from clairvoyant sight come from the location of the third eye, and as you will observe, they are of a completely different frequency from that of telepathy. It is in some ways the same type of thing giving different results. One might say that when you get telepathic messages you listen to radio, when you get clairvoyant messages you see television pictures, and often in glorious technicolor!

If you want to see clairvoyantly, you will need a crystal or something which shines. If you have a diamond ring with one stone, that is as good as a crystal and certainly it is less tiring to hold. Here again you will have to recline comfortably, and you will have to make sure that the lighting is of a very low order indeed. Let us assume, though, that you have invested in a crystal—

You are resting completely at ease in your room in the evening. Your curtains or blinds have been drawn to cut out any direct rays of light. The room is so dark that you can hardly see the outline of the crystal. It is so dark that you certainly cannot see any pinpoints of light in the crystal. Instead the whole thing is hazy, almost not there, you know that you are holding it, you know that you can see something. Keep looking into the crystal without trying to see anything, look into the crystal as if you were looking in the far far distance. This crystal will be just a few inches from you, but instead you have to look miles. Then you will see the crystal gradually begin to cloud, you will see white clouds form, and the crystal, instead of being apparently of clear glass, will appear to be full of milk. Now is the critical time, do not jerk, do not let yourself become alarmed, as so many people do, because the next stage—

The whiteness rolls away like curtains being drawn away to disclose a stage. Your crystal has gone—vanished—and you see instead the world. You are gazing down as a God on Olympus might look upon the world, you see perhaps the clouds with a continent beneath, you have a sensation of falling, you might even involuntarily jerk forward a little. Try to control this because if you do jerk, you will "lose the picture" and have to start all over again some other night. But supposing you did not jerk, then you will have the impression that you are speeding down and the world is getting larger and larger, you will find continents sweep beneath you, and then you will come to a halt at some particular spot. You might see a historical scene, you might even appear to land in the middle of a war and find a tank charging at you. There is nothing to be alarmed at in this because the tank cannot hurt you, it will go right through you and you will not know a thing about it. You may find that you are seeing apparently through the eyes of some other person, you cannot see the person's face, but you can see all that he or she would see.

Again, do not be alarmed, do not allow yourself to jerk, you will see quite clearly, quite plainly, and although you do not actually hear a sound, you will know everything that is being said. So it is that we see in clairvoyance. It is a very easy thing provided—again—that you have faith.

Some people do not actually see a picture, some people get all the impressions without actually seeing. This often happens to a person who is engaged in business. We can have a very clairvoyant person indeed, but if that person be engaged in business or commerce, then often there is a skeptical attitude which makes it difficult to actually see the picture, the person subconsciously thinks that such a thing cannot be, and as clairvoyance will not be completely denied, the person gets impressions "somewhere in the head" which are, nevertheless, as real as are the pictures.

With practice, you can see clairvoyantly. With practice, you can visit any period of the world's history and see what that history really was. You will be amused and amazed when you find most frequently that history was not as written in the history books, for history as written reflects the politics of the time. We can see how that happens in the case of Hitler, Germany, and Soviet Russia! Now let us deal with psychometry.

Psychometry can be termed "seeing through the fingers." Everyone has had some form of this experience, for instance, take a heap of coins and get some other person to hold just one of the coins for a few minutes. Then, if that coin is put back with the others, you will be able to pick the coin because it will be warmer than the rest. This, of course, is just an elementary little thing which has no place off the stage.

By psychometry we mean the ability to pick up an article and to know its origin, what has happened to it, who has had it and the person's state of mind. You can often get a sort of psychometry when you feel that an article has been in happy surroundings or unpleasant surroundings.

You can practice psychometry by enlisting the aid of a sympathetic friend. This is how you should set about it.

Assuming that your friend is sympathetic to you and wants to see you progress, we suggest that you get him to wash his hands and then pick up a stone or pebble. That also should be washed with soap and water and well rinsed. Then your friend should fully dry his hands and the stone, and then, holding the stone in his left hand, he should think strongly for about a minute; he should think of one thing—it can be of the color black, or white, or good temper, or bad temper, it does not matter what he thinks as long as he thinks strongly of one subject for about a minute. Having done that, he should wrap the stone in a clean handkerchief or a paper handkerchief, and hand it to you. You should not unwrap it then, but wait until you are alone in your "contemplation room." We are going to digress again!

We said with the left hand and let us first explain the reason. Under esoteric lore the right hand is supposed to be the practical hand, the hand devoted to the things of the world. The left hand is the spiritual hand, that which is devoted to metaphysical things. Provided that you are normally right-handed, then you will get greater results by using your left "esoteric" hand for psychometry. If you are one of those who are left-handed, then you will use your right hand in the metaphysical sense. It is to be observed that you can often get results with the left hand when you cannot with the right hand.

When you are in your room of contemplation, you will need to wash your hands very carefully, and then rinse them before drying them, because if you do not do that, you will have other impressions on your hands, and you want one impression only for this experiment.

Lie down, make yourself comfortable, and in this case it doesn't matter how much or how little light there is, you can have every light on or you can be in complete darkness. Then unwrap the stone or whatever it was, and pick it up with your left hand, see that it rolls into the center of your left palm. Do not think about it, do not bother about it, just try to let your mind go blank, think about nothing. You will next experience a very slight tingling in the left hand, and then you will get an impression, probably what your friend was trying to put over to you. You might also pick up the impression that he really thinks you are engaging upon a crackpot stunt! If you practice this, you will find that provided you are tranquil you can pick up most interesting impressions. When your friend is tired of assisting you, do it on your own, go out somewhere, get hold of a pebble which has not been touched by anyone so far as you know. This is easy if you are by a seashore, or you can dig up a stone from the earth. By practicing you will have truly remarkable results, you can, for example, pick up a pebble and know about the time when it was part of a mountain, how it was swept down by a river and out into the sea. The information that one can pick up by psychometry is truly amazing, but again, it needs a lot of practice, and you must keep your mind tranquil.

It is possible to pick up a letter which is still in an envelope and be aware of the general trend of the contents. It is also possible to pick up a letter written in a foreign language, and by running the finger tips of the left hand lightly over the surface, you will pick up the meaning of the letter even though you do not understand the individual words. This is quite infallible with practice, but never do it just to prove that you can do such a thing for the benefit of other people.

You may wonder why people will not prove that they are telepathic, that they are clairvoyant, etc. The answer is that when you are telepathic you have to have favorable conditions, you cannot do telepathy when you have someone trying to prove you wrong because you are picking up waves radiated by other people, and if you have a person close to you who is trying to prove you wrong, trying to say that you are a fake, then you will find that his radiations—perhaps of dislike and doubt and distrust—are so strong that they blank out weaker waves from afar. We recommend that if anyone asks you to give proof you tell them that you are not interested; you know, and what you know you do not have to prove to other people.

We would also like to say something about clairvoyants who live in back streets and make money therefrom. It is a fact that many women have great clairvoyant abilities off and on, that is, it is not constant, it cannot be switched on at will. There is frequently the case that a woman who is most talented at clairvoyance in brief flashes will astound her friends with true prophecies. They will suggest that she ought to take it up professionally. The poor deluded woman will do so, she will charge varying sums of money for her services. She cannot tell a client that today she does not feel that her clairvoyant ability is working, and so, in one of her blank times, she makes up something. She is usually a good psychologist, and as she gets into the habit of making up things she will find that her clairvoyant ability will recede.

You should never take money for reading the crystal or reading the cards. If you do, you will lose the ability to see clairvoyantly. You should never try to prove that you can do this or that, because if you do, you will be fairly blasted by the brain waves of those who disbelieve in you.

Oftentimes it is better not to admit how much you know. The more normal, the more natural you appear, the more you will pick up. We say never give proof, because if you try to give proof, you will be really inundated by doubt-waves from others who can cause great harm to you.

We ask you to practice and practice, and cultivate inner composure without which you cannot do any of these things. With inner composure and faith you can do anything!

Lesson Twenty-Two

BEFORE WE GO ON to our lesson proper, we should like to draw your attention to an item of very great interest which has just been drawn to our attention! It is of particular interest because throughout this course we have been talking so much about the electric currents of the body, and saying how currents travel along the nerves to activate the muscles. In *Electronics Illustrated* for January 1963, page 62, there is this fascinating article called "Russia's Amazing Electronic Hand." Professor Aron E. Kobrinsky is a Doctor of Engineering in the U.S.S.R. Academy of Sciences, and it seems that he, with his assistants—have been doing research into the matter of prosthetics—artificial limbs. Up to the present, the effort involved in making an artificial arm move at all has been a very tiring process for the wearer; now, however, in Russia there has been developed an artificial arm that is electrically operated.

At the time of the amputation, two special electrodes are put on the end of certain nerves, the nerves which normally would move the muscles of the arm, and when the stump has healed so that an artificial arm may be fitted, the currents coming from the brain down the nerves and which would normally move, say, fingers and thumb, are passed on to the artificial arm where the very minute body currents are amplified greatly so that relays may be operated and the fingers and thumb of the prosthetic appliance can work as did the natural finger and thumb. It is stated that with these artificial arms it is possible to write a letter. An illustration in *Electronics Illustrated* shows a person with an artificial arm holding a pencil between fingers and thumb, and actually writing.

You may have been a little tired of our discourse about electric currents, brain waves, etc., and that is why we mentioned this particular incident which really is most illuminating. We can visualize a future when all artificial appliances will be controlled by the "biochemical currents."

Now having dealt with that, we want to talk about emotions, because as we think so we are. If we think too much of sadness, then we start a process which results in certain of our body cells becoming corroded. Too much sadness, too much misery, can bring on liver complaints or gall bladder complaints. Consider this; a man and a woman married for a long time are very, very attached to each other. The man suddenly dies, and the woman, who is now a widow, is overcome with the desolation of her loss. She becomes prostrate with sadness, she becomes pale and may even waste away. Often there will actually be some severe physical illness. Worse, there may even be a mental breakdown. The cause of this is that under the violent stimulus of such a loss the brain generates a high current of electricity which floods through the body, penetrating all organs and all glands, and creating considerable back pressure. This inhibits the normal activities of the body. The sufferer may become numb, hardly able to think, hardly able to move. Frequently the excess stimulus at lachrymal glands will cause floods of tears because these glands act as a safety valve.

We get a similar sort of thing with the wrong voltage when we put, let us say, a 3.5 bulb in a 6 volt torch. Activity is very bright for a few moments and then the bulb blows out. The human body can "blow out" too, but that will result in trance, or coma, or even insanity.

Undoubtedly all of us have seen an animal that is very frightened. Possibly the animal has been chased by some larger fierce animal. The fugitive will not eat while it is frightened, and if one should be able to force that animal to eat, the food would not digest. All the gastric secretions which normally break down the food cease when an animal is frightened. Actually the secretions dry up. So, any intake of food is completely and utterly against the nature of the animal.

Very highly excited persons, or a person who is very depressed, should neither be persuaded nor forced to eat, for although no doubt such persuasion would be kindly meant, it would not be in the interests of the sufferer. Sorrow, or any deep emotion, brings a complete change in the chemical processes of the body. Uncertainty or sorrow can completely color a person's outlook, make a person unbearable, make a person impossible to get on with. When we say, "color a person's outlook," we mean just that, for one's chemical secretions really do alter the colors or the general trend of colors which one sees. We all know that those who are in love see the world through "rose-colored glasses," while those who are depressed and weary see the world through a definitely grayish tinge. If we are to make progress we must cultivate equanimity of temperament; we must attain such a balance of emotion that we are neither wildly excited nor unduly depressed. We must make sure that those brain waves which we talked about have no high peaks and no deep valleys. The human body is designed to function in a certain manner. All the fits and starts to which it is subjected in so-called civilization does definite harm. Proof of this can be seen in the number of business people who have gastric ulcers or heart attacks, or who become jumpy. Again, this is the result of high fluctuations of electricity creating that back pressure which we mentioned previously. The back pressure suffuses various organs and definitely interferes with their normal functioning. For instance, a person with ulcers—he does not take in food, and so the gastric acids become stronger and stronger, until in the end they literally burn a hole through him. It follows, then, that those who want to progress and do telepathy, clairvoyance, psychometry, and all the rest of it, must be sure indeed that they cultivate evenness of temperament. It can be cultivated!

Frequently a person will become moody, depressed, and uncertain. The person will be difficult indeed to live with. Any incident which another person would not notice, or, noticing, would laugh off, would irritate this nervous and moody person quite unbearably, and might even bring on an attack of hysteria or simulated suicide. Such things do happen! Do you know what hysteria is? It is a thing which actively is connected with the sex development of a person. Hysteria is connected with one of the most important female organs and functions, and often a woman will have a hysterectomy which sometimes affects her very badly by changing the whole functioning of the body. Many years ago, people had the belief that only women could have hysteria, but nowadays they are starting to know better, because every man is a bit of a woman, and every woman is a bit of a man, and the two are remarkably similar. It is now known that each sex has all the organs of the other in some degree or other. Hysteria, then, is now a man's complaint as well as that of a woman; hysteria is a great inhibitor of things to do with the occult. If a person gives way to moods and has wide fluctuations of electrical output from the brain, then that person will assuredly stop himself or herself from astral traveling, from telepathy, from clairvoyance, and from other metaphysical phenonema. We must be of even temperament; we have to be balanced before we can deal with the esoteric study. Remarkably enough, many people look upon clairvoyants or telepaths as being neurotic or imaginative, or something of that nature. They look upon the telepath and the clairvoyant as being unbalanced. Nothing could be further from the truth! Only the fake clairvoyant, only the fraudulent telepath can be neurotic or unbalanced because, as they are fakes and fraudulent anyhow, their state of mental health has no bearing on the subject. We say most definitely that one can only be telepathic, can only be clairvoyant, when the mind is functioning normally and the brain waves are fairly even and unruffled. The waves from the brain must be smooth that is, there must be no sudden peaks or depressions which will upset reception. We who are telepathic have to receive messages, therefore we have to be quiescent, we have to be receptive, which means that we have to keep our minds open. If our minds are in a furor all the time—if we are so busy thinking of our own miseries that we are not perceptive to the thoughts of others, then we shall not receive telepathically nor clairvoyantly. Again, the neurotic person cannot be clairvoyant genuinely. The psychopath is not a telepath!

Keep your mind free from upsets. When you feel irritated, or when you feel that the cares of the world are heaped upon your shuddering, sagging shoulders, take a deep breath, then take another and yet another. Think—will all these matters worry you in a hundred years time? Or will they worry anyone else in a hundred years time? If they are not going to worry you in a hundred years time, why should you worry about them now?

This business of keeping calm is of utter importance for health, both physical and mental, so we suggest that when you start to become irritable you come to a halt and ask yourself why you are feeling bad tempered? Why are you so gloomy, so miserable? Why are you upsetting the lives of other people around you? Remember, too, that in being gloomy, bad tempered, irritable, miserable, and all the gamut of bad emotions, you are hurting yourself only, you are not hurting the other person. He might be a bit tired of tantrums, but you are poisoning yourself as surely as if you took arsenic or rat poison or potassium cyanide! Some of the people around you probably have far greater problems than you, yet they are not showing the effect of strain. If you are showing the effects of strain, it means that you do not have the correct perspective, it means that possibly—not inevitably—you may not be of the same mental and spiritual status as the other person.

We are upon Earth to learn, and no normal human is ever given too much to learn at one time. We may feel that we are being persecuted, victimized, we may feel that we are the subject of an unkind malignant fate, yet if we really reflect upon the matter we can see that we are not overstressed, we only think that we are. Let us get back to children again; a child may be given homework. He may think that there is a shocking amount of homework, especially as he wants to go out playing games or fishing, or chasing after a member of the opposite sex. He is so busy thinking of playing games and fishing that he does not even devote the normal one-tenth of his mind to his work, and so it appears to be hard. Because he is making no real effort to get through his work, he finds that it takes far longer than it would for any thinking person. He gets tired of the work, he does not devote a twentieth of his consciousness to the work, and he becomes more and more frustrated. Eventually he complains to his parents that he has too much homework, that all the strain is making him ill. The parents complain to the teacher that the child has too much work to do. No one thinks of talking some sense to the child who, after all, is the one who should be trained! As with the child, so with you. You want to make progress? Then you have to abide by certain rules, you have to keep calm, you have to take the middle way. If you work too hard, you are so busy thinking about the hard work that you are putting in that you have no time to think out the results you hope to obtain. So— the middle way is a very simple means of telling you that you must not work so hard, if you cannot "see the forest for the trees." You must not laze so much that nothing at all is done; go somewhere between the extremes and you will find that your progress is remarkable. Too many people really slave at a thing in the hope of getting it done, they try so hard that all their energy, all their brain power is devoted to "trying," and nothing is left for "attaining." If you try too hard, it's like a car racing along in low gear, all fuss and splutter, and making hardly any progress.

The Power of the Mind

It is unfortunately possible for anyone to have anything that one wants. There are certain laws of nature, or, if you prefer, of esoteric study, which makes it possible for anyone to have success or money if you will follow simple rules. We have tried to show throughout this course that occultism, which really means "that which is hidden," follows absolutely sensible laws and rules, and that there is nothing mystical about such things. For that purpose we are going to tell you how to get what you want!

Let us say, though, that when we say, "Get what you want," we emphasize and reemphasize that you should strive for the spiritual values, you should at all times work with determination to increase your worth in the next life. A million or two would be very useful, let us hasten to agree on that, but it would be a snare and a delusion if we had a million or two at the expense of the next life. Our stay on Earth is temporary, and again we state that every effort upon this Earth should be devoted to learning and to improving ourselves so that we are worth more when we move into the next life. Let us, then, strive for spirituality, let us strive that we may show kindness to others, and that true humility, which must not be confused with false modesty, but the humility which assists us on the climb upward.

Everything is in a state of movement, all life is movement, even death is movement, because cells are breaking down and turning into other compounds. Let us remember at all times that one cannot stand still on a tightrope, one can either go forward or backward. Our endeavors should be to go forward, that is, we should move forward into spirituality, into kindness, into understanding for others, not backward where we should be among the money-grabbers, those who cling to temporal possessions rather than striving to attain richness of the spirit. But—let us show you how you may gain all you desire.

The mind can give us all that we ask if we will let it. There are immense powers latent within the subconscious. Unfortunately most people are not taught how to contact the subconscious. We function at one-tenth consciousness, and— at most—one-tenth of abilities. By aligning the subconscious on our side we can achieve miracles as did the Prophets of old.

It is useless to pray idly and without being specific. It is useless to pray with an empty mind because your words will echo hollowly if you do so. Use your brain, use your mind, use the great possibilities of the subconscious. There are certain inviolable steps which always must be followed. First decide precisely what you want, be absolutely definite, you must know what you want, you must say what you want, and you must visualize it. WHAT EXACTLY DO YOU WANT? It will not do to say you want a lot of money, it will not do to say that you want a new car or a new wife or a new husband. You must state EXACTLY what it is that you want. You must visualize it—picture it in your mind—and hold that picture firmly before you. If you want money, state quite definitely how much you want. It must be a definite sum. "About half a million" will not do, it must be definite. If you are wise, however, you will not bother so much about money, about the mundane things, you will want to be like Gandhi, Buddha, Christ, St. Peter, St. Anybody. You will strive to gain virtues which will be of use to you when you leave this life.

When you have decided what you want you come to stage two. We have already told you that you must give in order that you may receive. What are you going to give? If you are asking for a certain sum of money (and that sum must be exactly specified) are you willing to give a tithe, which, of course, is a tenth, of that money? Are you willing to give help to other people who are not so fortunately placed as you? It is futile to say "Yes, when I get this money I will give a tenth of it." You must start helping before that, you must start assisting those in need. If you do that, you will be living the spirit of, "Give that you may receive." Again, you must be definite, you must be absolutely precise. The third item is— when do you want this money or this car, or new husband or new wife? It is not enough to say that you want it sometime in the indefinite future, and of course it is absurd to say that you want it immediately because there are physical laws which cannot be broken. It is not possible for a God to drop a gold brick into your waiting hands, and in any case if the brick did fall it would probably crush a few toes! Your time limit must be physically feasible. You could, for instance, say that you will have the money by such-and-such a month in such-and-such a year, but you could not say that you would have a fortune within the next five minutes because that would be contrary to the laws of nature, and it would nullify your thought power.

What are you going to do to realize your ambition? Supposing—just by way of illustration—that you want a new car. Well, first of all, can you drive? It would be of little point to

208 T. Lobsang Rampa

want a new car unless you know how to drive, so if you are determined to have a new car, take driving lessons first. Then you can decide on the type of car you want, and all that sort of thing. If you are looking for a husband or a wife make sure that you in your turn are fitted to be an adequate partner, make sure that you understand the law of give and take and are prepared to do your share to make a success of marriage, because marriage is not just a case of take all and give naught. When you take a partner you also have to give a partner to the other person. When you get married, you cease to be one person, and you take on the problems and the worries and the pleasures of two persons; before you can hope to be satisfactorily and happily married, you have to be sure that you are able physically, mentally, and spiritually to be a satisfactory partner yourself.

As our fifth item we are going to say that the written word is stronger than the spoken word, while the two together make an unbeatable combination. Write out what you want, write it out as simply and as clearly as you can. You know what you want, so write it down. Do you want to be spiritual? Who is your ideal in the world of spirituality? Enumerate that person's abilities, talents, and strong points of character.Write it all down. If you are trying to get money, write down the precise sum you want, write down when you want it, and make clear in writing that you are going to help other people, make clear that you are going to tithe. When you have written all this down as simply and as clearly as you can, write at the end "I will give that I may receive." You must also add a note stating how you are going to work for the desired result, for bear in mind once again that you cannot get anything for nothing, everything has to be paid for in some form or other, there is no such thing as getting something for free. If you receive a hundred dollars unexpectedly you have to give a hundred dollars worth of service. If you expect other people to help you, then you must first help them.

Assuming that you have written all this down, read your statement aloud to yourself three times a day. There is power gained if you can read it aloud in the quietude and privacy of your own room. Read it in the morning before you leave your bedroom, read it at lunch time, and read it once again before going to sleep at night so that three times a day, at least, you have read your affirmation which has thus become akin to a mantra. As you read this, FEEL that the money or car, or whatever it is that you want, is coming to you, be positive about it, imagine that you have the thing desired, imagine that it is actually within your grasp. The stronger you can think about this, that you can imagine all this, the more positive will the reaction be. It is a waste of effort to think, "Well, I only hope it works—I only hope I shall get it, but I have my doubts." That will invalidate your mantra immediately, you must be quite positive and absolutely constructive all the time, and you must not permit any doubts to enter. If you will adopt these steps, you will drive the thought into your subconscious, and the subconscious is nine times cleverer than you are! If you can interest your subconscious, then you will get help, more help than you believed possible. It is a fact proved time after time that when one makes money, other money comes more easily. A millionaire, for instance, would tell you that after he made one million, two, three, or four million came very much more easily and with little additional work. The more money you have, the more money is attracted to you, it works on the law akin to that of magnetism.

Again let us caution you that there are things of greater value than money. Once again let us say that no one has ever taken a single coin into the next world, and the more money you have the more you leave for other people, the more you strive for money, the more you contaminate yourself, and make it difficult for yourself to aspire and to attain to the spiritual values. The more good you do for others, the more good you take away with you. Life on Earth is hard, and one of the hardest things of all is the falsification of values. At the present time people think that money is all that matters. So long as we have enough that we may eat, clothe ourselves and be sheltered, that will suffice. But we can never have too much spirituality, we can never have too much purity of thought, we can never help others too much, for in helping others we help ourselves.

We suggest that you read and reread this lesson. Perhaps it is the most important lesson yet. If you follow the instruction, you will find that you can have almost anything you want. What do *you* want? The choice must be yours, for you *can* have whatever it is that you desire. A pointer—money, success on this Earth? And then eclipse and a start all over again. Or will you choose spirituality, purity, and service to others? It may mean poverty or near-poverty on the Earth, which, after all, is only a speck of dust floating in the void. But after this short, short life there comes the greater world where purity and spirituality is the "Coin of the Realm," and where money, the currency of the world of Earth, has no value. The choice is yours!

Lesson Twenty-Three

IT IS MOST regrettable that certain words have acquired such an unsavory connotation. There are a number of words which are good words, descriptive words, in all languages, but which through misuse throughout perhaps centuries have undergone a complete change of meaning.

We could refer to the word "mistress" as an illustration. Just a few years ago within the memory of our grandparents—the word "mistress" was an honorable one indicating a lady who was to be respected as mistress of the household, the lady of the house, a fit partner for the man of the house. By misuse it has now acquired a meaning which is altogether different from that which it originally possessed.

We are not going to talk about old mistresses, nor old masters, but it seemed an appropriate example because we are going to talk in this lesson about another word, the meaning of which has become distorted throughout the years.

Imagination is a word which now is in sore disgrace. Years ago a man of imagination was a man of sensitive ideas, one who could write, one who could compose music or poetry. It was, in fact, absolutely essential for a gentleman to be possessed of imagination. Nowadays it appears that imagination indicates some poor frustrated woman suffering from hysteria or on the verge of a mental breakdown. People brush off experiences—which they would far better study—with the exclamation, "Oh, it's all your imagination! Don't be so silly!"

Imagination, then, is a word that is in poor repute today, but controlled imagination is a key that can unlock many experiences which are at present locked in the veil of mystery which surrounds most people when they refer to occult matters. It is well to remember time and time again that in any battle between the imagination and the will it is always the imagination that wins. People pride themselves upon their will power, upon their indomitable courage, upon the fact that nothing frightens them. They assure bored listeners that with their will power they can do anything at all. The whole truth of the matter is that with will power they can do nothing unless the imagination agrees to permit it. These people of much-vaunted will power are actually those who have managed somehow (usually by accident) to let the imagination believe that a good dose of "will power" would be useful in this particular instance. We repeat, and any competent authority will agree with us, that in the matter of imagination and will power, it is without exception imagination that wins. There is no greater power.

Do you still doubt that you can will yourself to do things when your imagination does not want you to? Consider this; let us pose a hypothetical problem because that appears to be the modern way of doing things.

We have before us a street devoid of traffic. There is no traffic about, there are no curious sightseers, so we have the whole street to ourselves. Let us paint a path some two or three feet wide, if you prefer—from one sidewalk to the other. Undisturbed by the thought of avoiding traffic, or unperturbed by the curious stares of onlookers, you would have not the slightest difficulty nor hesitation in stepping off one sidewalk onto your two or three foot wide path and walk sedately across the road to the other sidewalk. This would not cause your breath rate to increase, it would not cause your heart to flutter, it would be one of the simplest things you had ever been called upon to do. Will you agree with us so far?

You can walk along the painted pathway without a thought of fear because you know that the ground is not going to give way beneath you, you know that except in the case of an earthquake or a building falling over on top of you, you are quite safe, and if by some singular misfortune you should trip and fall to the ground, no great harm would be done because you cannot fall further than your own height.

Now let us alter the picture somewhat. Let us say that we are still in the street, and we move to a building which is about twenty stories high. We will get into the elevator and move upward, up to the beautifully flat roof. As we stand on the roof and we look across the street, we observe that we are quite level with another building twenty stories high just across from us. If we look over the wall and down at the roadway beneath we can just see the painted line that we made. Now, we are going to have a board two or three feet wide, in other words, a board precisely as wide as was our painted line. We will stretch it across the street, twenty stories high across the street, and we will anchor it so firmly that it cannot move; we will anchor it so securely that it cannot sway or bounce, we will examine it most carefully to see that there is nothing at all which could trip you or make your footsteps uncertain.

You have the same width of pathway as you did on ground level. Can you walk across that plank which is fixed securely twenty stories above the street, and reach the other side of the street—reach the roof of the other building? If your imagination says you can, then indeed you can and without any great trouble. But if your imagination is not so complaisant then your pulse will race at the mere thought of it, you will feel "butterflies in the stomach," you might even feel worse than that! But why? You have already walked across the road, so why can you not walk across this beautifully firm board? The answer is, of course, that your imagination starts working, your imagination tells you that here is danger, that if you slip, if you falter, you will step off the edge of the board you will fall twenty stories down to destruction. It does not matter how much one tries to reassure you, unless your imagination can be assured, no amount of will power can help. If you try to assert your will power, you might have a nervous breakdown, you will start to tremble, you will turn pale and your breath will come in stertorous gasps.

We have certain mechanisms built into us which protect us from danger, certain automatic safeguards are built into the human mechanism so that a human cannot normally run into foolish danger. Imagination makes it almost impossible for a person to walk the plank, and no amount of telling would enable a person to realize that it really was perfectly safe, you need to imagine that you can do it. Until you really can "imagine" yourself stepping up to the plank, getting onto it, and walking firmly and confidently across, then you cannot do it.

If one wills oneself to do a thing when the imagination says "No," then one does indeed risk a nervous breakdown, for we are going to repeat once again that in any battle between the imagination and the will power, the imagination always wins. Forcing ourselves to do something when all the alarm signals are clanging within us can wreck one's nerves, wreck one's health.

Some people are desperately afraid of passing a graveyard on a lonely road at midnight. If the occasion arises when they have to pass a cemetery at night, they feel their scalp tingle, their hair stands on end, their palms begin to perspire, and every perception is heightened, every impression is exaggerated, and they are indeed keyed up to make a prodigious leap to safety should the appearance of a ghost apparently call for escape.

People who do not like their work and have to force themselves to do their work, often bring into use an escape mechanism. Some of these "escape mechanisms" lead to rather weird results, they may be blessings in disguise because if warnings are not heeded mental breakdowns can occur. We are going to relate an actual instance which is well known to us, we know the instance, we know the man, and we know the result. Here it is:—

This man of our acquaintance did a lot of standing. He stood at one of those tall desks and entered figures in a ledger. His work was such that he had to stand, the work could not be done easily sitting down. The man was competent at his job, he was good at these figures, but he had a phobia; he was truly desperately afraid that someday, somehow he would make a mistake and perhaps be accused of embezzling a sum of money from his employers. Actually the man was painfully honest, he was one of those rare individuals who make hard work of honesty, one of those individuals who would not even take a book of matches from a hotel and would not keep a newspaper that he found on a bus seat. But even so, he was afraid that his employers did not know of his honesty, and that made him feel very bad indeed about his work.

For a number of years he went about the work becoming more and more unhappy, more and more preoccupied. He discussed a change of work with his wife, but she had no sympathy with him, and so he kept to the same job. But his imagination got to work also; first the man got gastric ulcers. With careful attention and diet those ulcers were cured, and he returned to work—returned to standing at a desk. It occurred to him one day that if he did not have the ability to stand then he would not have the ability to keep that job.

Some weeks later an ulcer appeared on his foot. For a few days he hobbled to work and endured great pain, but the ulcer got worse, and he had to remain in bed for a time. Being in bed—being away from his office, his recovery was quite speedy, and then he went back to work. All the time his subconscious mind was nagging him. It reasoned, one supposed, something like this: "Well, I got out of that horrible job by having a foot complaint, they cured me too quickly so let me have a worse foot complaint." A few months after the man's return, presumably cured, he got another ulcer, this time on the ankle. It was such a bad ulcer that he could not move his ankle. Eventually he was taken to the hospital, and as the ulcer became worse and worse and he had to have an operation. After this he was discharged cured, and went back to his job.

Now the hatred of the job was growing on him. Soon another ulcer appeared, this time between the ankle and the knee, this time it was so bad—resisting all efforts to cure it—that he had to have his leg amputated at the knee. This time to his great joy the employer would not have him back, saying that he would not have a cripple around, a cripple who was always falling sick!

The doctors at the hospital knew quite a lot about this case, and so they arranged for the man to do some other work, work for which he had shown considerable aptitude while in the hospital. It was a form of handicraft instruction. He liked the work and had much success at it. There was now no fear that he would go to prison for some mistake which would cause him to be accused of embezzling, so his health improved, and, so far as is known at the present time, he is carrying on this work and making a success at it.

This is rather an extreme case, true, but every day we see high-pressured businesspeople who are in fear of their jobs, in fear of their employers, or in fear of "losing face," working at high internal pressures and then seeking to escape by way of gastric ulcers. Gastric ulcers, in fact, are known as the executives complaint.

Imagination can topple an empire, imagination can build an empire as well, remember. If you will cultivate your imagination and control it, you can have whatever you want. It is not possible to dictate to your imagination, not possible to tell it what it shall do because Friend Imagination is something like Friend Mule; you can lead a mule but you cannot drive him, and so you can lead your imagination but you cannot drive it. It needs practice, but it can be done.

Well, how are you going to set about controlling your imagination? It is only a matter of faith, of practice. Think of some situation which excites your fear or your distaste, and then overcome it by faith, by persuading your imagination that you can do a thing no matter what others can or cannot do. Persuade yourself that you are some special sort of being, if you like, it does not matter what method you adopt for yourself so long as you get your imagination working on your behalf. Let us revert to our original illustration about crossing the street, let us decide that we can easily cross the street on a two foot plank resting across the roadway. Then, by faith, by thinking that we are not as others, we can persuade our imagination that we can cross the plank even though it be elevated twenty stories above the ground.

Think of this—Tell yourself that even a more or less brainless monkey can cross that plank with no fear at all. Who is better, you or a brainless monkey? If a brainless monkey or a person who is almost an idiot can cross that plank, then surely you, a much better person, can do so also. It is merely a question of practice, of having faith. In the past there have been famous tightrope walkers such as Blondin, who crossed a rope many times over the Niagara Falls. Blondin was just an ordinary man who had faith in his abilities, he had faith that he could cross where other men could not. He knew that the only thing to be afraid of was of being afraid; he knew that if he was confident of going across, then he could cross no matter if he was pushing a wheelbarrow or if he was blindfolded.

We all get the same sort of experience. We climb up a long ladder, and as long as we look up, we experience no fear. But as soon as we look down the thought occurs to us that we would make an awfully bad mess if we fell off the ladder and then crashed. Our imagination then pictures ourselves falling, pictures us being smeared many feet below, our imagination might picture us clinging so tightly to that ladder that we cannot free ourselves. Steeplejacks have had that type of experience!

If you control your imagination by building up faith in your own abilities, you can do anything. You cannot succeed in overcoming your imagination by force, exercising your will power will not overcome your imagination, it will instead build up a neurosis within you. Remember, once again, that you must at all times lead your imagination, control your imagination. If you try to drive your imagination, you will fail. If you will lead your imagination, you will be able to do all those things which you thought would be impossible for you. First of all, though, believe that there is no such thing as impossible.

Lesson
Twenty-Four

PEOPLE MAY HAVE heard of the law of karma. Fortunately so many of these metaphysical matters have been given Sanskrit or Brahmin names. In much the same way medical terms, anatomical terms, and, in fact, many scientific terms, have Latin names, Latin names can indicate a type of flower, or a bulb, or the action of a particular muscle or artery. The purpose of this originated in the days of long ago. Many years ago, doctors tried to keep their knowledge to themselves, and the doctors of those days were the only ones who had any worthwhile education.

There are certain advantages, of course, in having technical terms all in one language, because it doesn't matter what is the native language of a scientist, he can still manage quite well by discussing things with a foreign scientist in Latin.

Radio operators aboard ship or on aircraft have much the same idea when they use Morse code or what is known as the "Q" code. Often you will find that radio amateurs who keep in touch with other amateurs throughout the world use code so that they can communicate intelligently even though they normally will not understand a word of each other's language.

Sanskrit is a language which is known to advanced occult-ists throughout the world, so that if one refers to "karma," one gets a particular picture of what we could term "the law of cause and effect." You see, karma is nothing at all mysterious, nothing at all frightening. In this course we want to put meta-physics upon what we consider to be a rational basis, we do not want to use abstract terms because to our way of thinking nothing in metaphysics is so difficult as to warrant the use of terms which often actually conceal one's meaning.

Let us take the "Law of Karma" out of its metaphysical connotation, let us forget about metaphysics, and let us instead consider the law of the land. Here is what we mean:—

Little Johnny So-and-So has just been given a motorcycle. He finds that there is a great thrill in sitting on this powerful machine and letting the engine race and make what is to him a wondrous noise, but sitting upon the machine is not good enough. Little Johnny So-and-So lets in the clutch and rides away, sedately perhaps at first, but then the joy of movement overcomes him and he goes faster and faster, oblivious of warning signs. Suddenly there is a blaring hoot behind him and a police car pulls up alongside and motions him into the curb. Little Johnny So-and-So glumly slows down and pulls off the road, even more glumly he waits with considerable apprehension for the policeman who is going to give him a ticket for going far above the permitted speed limit in a resi-dential area.

In this simple example, we have seen that there are cer-tain laws, in this case the law was that no one could travel at more than a certain speed. Johnny So-and-So ignored that and so retribution in the form of a policeman came along and gave him a ticket so that Johnny So-and-So would have to pay a fine and go to court as punishment for having broken the law.

Another example? All right! Bill James is a bit of a lazy fellow, he doesn't like work at all, but he has a very expensive girl friend. He can only keep his girl friend's interest so long as he can provide her with the things that she wants. It doesn't matter to her (she thinks) how Bill James gets the things she wants, so long as she gets them. So—

One evening Bill James sets out with the intention of robbing some store in the hope of obtaining enough money so that he can buy his girl friend whatever it is that she wants. A mink coat? A platinum diamond-studded watch? Well, no matter what she wants, Bill James, with her full knowledge and approval, sets out to do this burglary. Very silently he creeps up to the building and prowls around seeking for some mode of entry. Soon he decides that he will get in what appears to be quite an inviting window. It is at a convenient height for him, so with the skill of much practice he slides a penknife through the window panes and forces back the catch. Easily he raises the sash, and then stops for a moment to listen. Has he made any noise? Is anyone about? Satisfied at last, he eases himself up and crawls through the open window. There is not a sound, not a creak. Quietly in stocking feet he pads through the store taking the things he wants, jewelry from cases, a pocketful of watches, and from a cash box in the manager's office he takes quite a pile of bills. Satisfied with his loot, he creeps back to the window and looks out. There is no one there, he retrieves his shoes and makes his way to a door, thinking that it would be so much easier to get out of a door than to creep through a window and possibly damage some of the stolen articles. Silently he eases back the bolts and walks out. A few steps into the darkness of the night and a sudden harsh voice says, "Stop! I have you covered!" Bill James freezes with fright, he knows the police are armed, he knows the police will not hesitate to shoot. A light pierces the darkness and shines full upon his face. Glumly he raises his hands above his head, figures materialize and he finds that he is surrounded by police. Quickly they search him for weapons and relieve him of all the very valuable items which he had stolen from the store. He is led off to a waiting police car and is soon ensconced in a cell.

Some hours later the girl friend is awakened from her sleep by a policeman and a police matron. She is very, very indignant and not a little hysterical when she is told that she is to be arrested. Arrested? Yes, of course, for Bill James girl friend was an accessory before the fact, and she, by inciting him to do that which he knew was wrong, is as much guilty as he is.

The laws of life are like that. Now let us take it away from the physical world for a moment and tell you that karma is a mental or physical act which builds up good or bad. There is an old saying, "As ye sow so shall ye reap." It means just that. If you are going to sow bad deeds you will reap a bad future either in the next life, or the next, or the one after that. If in this life you sow good, if you show goodness and kindness and compassion to those in need, then when your own turn comes to have misfortune, someone—somewhere—will show you kindness and consideration and compassion.

Make no mistake about this; if a person is suffering hardship now it may be because that person is evil, it may be to see how the person reacts under hardship, under suffering, it may be a process of refining to drive away by suffering some of the impurities, some of the selfishness of humanity. Everyone, be he prince or beggar, travels along what we call the Wheel of Life, the circle of endless existence. A man may be king in one life, but in the next he may be a beggar traveling a-foot from city to city, perhaps trying to get work and failing, or perhaps just drifting along like a leaf blowing before a gale.

There are some people who are exempt from the laws of karma, so it is useless for you to say, "Oh, what a terrible life that person has had, he must have been a terrible sinner in a previous life!" The higher entities (whom we call Avatars) come down to Earth in order that certain tasks may be accomplished. The Hindus, for instance, believe that the God Vishnu descends onto Earth at various times in order to bring to mankind once again the truths of religion which mankind is so prone to forget. This Avatar, or Advanced Being, will often come to live, perhaps, as an example of poverty, but to show what can be done in the way of compassion, in the way of what seems to be immunity to suffering. Nothing could be further from the truth about this "immunity to suffering," for the Avatar, being of finer material, suffers the more acutely.

The Avatar is not born because he has to be, he is not born that he may work out his karma. Instead he comes to Earth as an embodied soul, his birth is the result of free choice, or under certain conditions he may not even be born, he may take over the body of another. We do not want to tread on anyone's toes in the matter of religious beliefs, but if one will read the Christian Bible closely, one will understand that Jesus, the man, was born of Joseph and Mary, but in the fullness of time and when Jesus was a grown man, Jesus wandered into the wilderness and the Spirit of Christ—the Spirit of God—descended and filled the body of Jesus. In other words, it was a case that another soul came and possessed the willing body of Jesus, the son of Joseph and Mary.

We mention this, though, because we do not like to think that some people are being blamed for misfortunes and poverty when actually they come to help others by showing what may be accomplished by misfortune and poverty.

Everything we do results in some action. Thought is a very real force indeed. As you think, so you are. Thus, if you think of pure things you become pure, if you think of lust then you become lustful and contaminated, and you have to come back to Earth time after time until desire withers within you under the onslaught of purity and good thinking.

No person is ever destroyed, no person is ever so bad that he or she is condemned to everlasting punishment. The everlasting punishment was a device started by the priests of old who wanted to maintain discipline over their somewhat unruly flock. Christ never taught eternal suffering, eternal damnation. Christ taught that if a person repented and tried, then a person would be "saved" from his or her own folly and given a chance and a chance again.

Karma, then, is the process whereby we incur debts and we pay off those debts. If you go into a store and you order certain goods, then you are incurring certain debts which have to be paid for in the coin of the realm. Until you have paid for those goods you are a debtor, and if you do not pay for the articles you can, in some countries, be arrested to be made a bankrupt. Everything has to be paid for by the ordinary man, woman and child upon the Earth, only the Avatar is immune from the laws of karma. So those who are not Avatars had better try to lead a good life so that they may cut short their sojourn on this Earth, for there is much better on other planets and on other planes of existence.

We should forgive those that trespass against us, and we should seek the forgiveness of those against whom we trespass. We should always remember that the surest way to a good karma is to do to others as we would have them do to us.

Karma is a matter which few of us can escape. We make a debt, we have to pay it, we do good to others, they must pay us back and do good to us. It is much better for us to receive good, so let us show good, compassion and kindness to all creatures, no matter what their species, remembering that in the eyes of God all people are equal, and in the eyes of Great God all creatures are equal whether they be cats, horses—what will you call them?

God, it is stated, works in a mysterious way His wonders to perform. It is not for us to question the ways of God, but it is for us to work out the problems allotted to us, for only in working out our problems and bringing them to a satisfactory conclusion can we pay off karma. Some people have a sick relative with whom they must live, some people have this sick relative living with them and they think, "Oh, how tiresome! Why cannot he die and be out of his misery?" The answer is, of course, that both are working out a planned life span, working out a planned form of existence. The person who is looking after the sick one may have planned to come just for that purpose.

We should at all times show great care, great concern, great understanding for those who are ill, or sorrowing, or are afflicted, for it may be that our task is to show such care and such understanding. It is too easy to brush off a tiresome person with an impatient gesture, but those who are sick are most frequently very highly sensitive, they feel their disabilities, they feel very keenly that they are in the way, not wanted. We would again remind you that as things are on Earth at present every person who is truly occult, every person who can do the major occult arts has some physical disability. Thus, in spurning, in rudely brushing off an appeal for help from some sick person, you may be brushing off a person who is far, far more gifted than you can ever imagine.

We have no interest in football or any of those strenuous sports, but we do want to ask you this question. Have you ever heard of a strong, rugged sportsman or sportswoman who was clairvoyant? The process of some physical disability is often a process of refining a gross human body so that it can receive vibrations of a higher frequency than can the average human. So—show consideration to those who are sick, will you? Do not be impatient with a sick person, for the sick person has many problems with which you are unacquainted. There is a selfish side to it too! The sick person may be far more evolved than are you who are healthy, and in helping that sick person you could indeed help yourself immensely.

Lesson Twenty-Five

HAVE YOU EVER been suddenly, devastatingly, shockingly deprived of a dearly loved one? Have you ever felt that the Sun had retreated behind the clouds, never, never to shine for you again? The loss of one who is dear indeed is tragic, tragic for you, and tragic for the one who has "gone on before" if you keep on making unnecessary drags—

We are going to talk about subjects which are usually regarded as sad, as gloomy, in this lesson. But if we regarded things as we should, we should perceive that death is not really a time for mourning, not really a time for sorrowing.

Let us have a look first at what happens when we are aware that a loved one has passed on to that stage which people of Earth call "death." We are going along in our normal way, possibly untroubled by any care or by any vexation.

Then, suddenly, like a bolt from the blue, we are informed that this dearly beloved person is no longer with us. Immediately we feel our pulse race, we feel that the lachrymal ducts of our eyes get ready to shed moisture to relieve the tension within. We find that no longer do we see bright rosy cheerful colors, instead everything looks gloomy, everything looks sad as though suddenly a bright summer's day had been replaced by one of complete midwinter with leaden overcast skies.

Once again we come to our old friends the electrons, for when we are suddenly afflicted with sadness, with grief, the voltage generated in our brains alters, it may even change its direction of flow so that if we were seeing the world "through rose colored glasses" before, then after the receipt of the sad news we see the world through glasses which make everything gloomy, everything depressing. That is just a natural physiological function in the mundane plane, but in the astral plane we are depressed also because of the horrible drag which our physical vehicle gives us when we try to go to greet the one who is newly arisen into what is, after all, the Greater Life, the happier life.

It is sad indeed to have a loved friend go off to a far distant country, but upon Earth we console ourselves with the thought that we can always write a letter, send a cable, or even use a telephone. So-called "death" on the other hand does not appear to leave any room for communication. Do you think that the dead are beyond reach? You could be greatly and joyously mistaken! We say to you that there are various scientists in reputable scientific centers of the world who are actually working on an instrument which will be capable of communicating with those to whom we must refer as "disembodied spirits." This is not a pipe dream, it is not a fantastic thought, it is an item of news which has been bruited about for quite a number of years, and according to the latest scientific reports there is at last some hope that such developments may soon become public knowledge, public property.

But before we can get in touch with those who have passed beyond our immediate reach we can do much to help them.

When a person dies, the physiological functions, that is, the actual workings of the physical body, slow down and eventually stop. We have seen in the preliminary stages of this course that a human brain can live for only minutes when deprived of oxygen. The human brain, then, is one of the first portions of the body to "die." Obviously when the brain is dead, death is utterly inevitable. We have a special reason for making this what appears to be a long drawn out affair.

After the death of the brain, other organs deprived of the commands and the guidance of the brain subside into quiescence, that is, they become like a motor car which has been deserted by the driver. The driver has switched off the ignition and left the vehicle. The engine may give a few kicks over by its own momentum, and then gradually the car will cool. As it cools one will get little clicks and grunts and squeaks from contracting metal. The same with the human body; as one organ follows another into that stage which we call dissolution, there are various creaks and grunts and twitches of muscles. Over a period of some three days the astral body completely and permanently disengages its hold of the physical body. The silver cord which we may say roots the astral body to the physical, gradually withers in much the same way as the umbilical cord of a baby withers when cut, when the baby is separated from the mother. For three days the astral body is kept in more or less close contact with the decaying physical.

A person who has died has an experience something like this; the person is in bed, possibly surrounded by sorrowing relatives or friends. There comes a shuddering gasp in the throat, and the final rattle of death, and then the last harsh breath is exhaled through the teeth. The heart races for a moment, slows, flutters, and stops—permanently.

There are various tremors of the body, gradually the body becomes colder, but at the instant of death itself, a clairvoyant can see a shadowy form emerge from the physical vehicle and float upward like a silvery mist, float up to lie directly above the dead body. Over a period of three days, the silver cord connecting the two darkens, eventually it turns black where it enters the body. Then one gets an impression of black dust flying off that part of the cord which is still connected to the body. At last the cord drops loose and the astral form is free to rise properly and to get its introduction to the life above the astral. First, though, it has to look down and see this dead body which it used to inhabit. Often the astral form will accompany a hearse to the cemetery and will actually witness the funeral proceedings. There is no pain, no distress, no upset caused by this because the astral, in the case of a person unprepared by knowledge such as that contained within this course, is in a state of semi-shock. It follows the body in the coffin in much the same way as a kite will follow a small boy at the other end of a string, or in much the same way as a balloon follows the trailer car which holds it from escaping. Soon, though, this silver cord—silver no longer—parts, and then the astral body is free to go up and up, and to prepare for its second death. This second death is completely and absolutely painless.

Before the second death, a person has to go to the Hall of Memories and see all that happened in this life. You are not judged by anyone except yourself, and there is no greater judge, no sterner judge than yourself. When you see yourself stripped of all the petty conceits, all the false values that were dear to you upon the Earth you may find that in spite of all the money you have left behind, in spite of all the positions you have held, all the appointments, you are not so great after all. Very, very frequently the most humble, the most lowly and the poorest in money, get the most satisfactory and highest judgment.

After having seen yourself in the Hall of Memories, then you go on to that portion of the "Other World" which you think is most suitable for you. You do not go to Hell, believe us when we say that Hell is upon Earth—our training school!

You will probably know that people in the East, great mystics, great teachers, never let their true name be known because there is much power in names, and if all and sundry can call upon one in the correct vibration of one's name, then one is pulled irresistibly back to gaze upon the Earth. In some parts of the East, and in some parts of the West, too, God is known as "He whose name may not be spoken." That is because if everyone kept calling on God, then the leader of this world would have a most harrowing time.

Many teachers adopt a name which is not their own, a name which differs markedly from the pronunciation of their true name, for names, remember, consist of vibrations, of chords and harmonies, and if one is called by what is one's own harmonic combination of vibrations, then one is greatly distracted from any work which one may be doing at the time.

Sorrowing unduly for those who have "passed over" causes them pain, causes them to feel dragged down to the Earth. They are much the same as a man who has been cast into the water and feels himself dragged down by soggy clothes and heavy boots.

Let us consider again this matter of vibrations, for vibration is the essence of life upon this Earth, and in fact upon any and all worlds. We all know a very simple illustration of the power of vibration; soldiers who are marching along keeping step will break back that step and walk across a big bridge in any disordered array of paces. The bridge may be capable of withstanding the heaviest mechanized traffic, it may be capable of bearing a whole succession of armored tanks rattling across, or it may bear a whole load of railway locomotives, and it will not deviate more than its designated amount through that load. Yet let a column of men march in step across that bridge, and it will set up a momentum that causes the bridge to sway and bounce, and eventual1y to collapse.

Another illustration we might give in the matter of vibration is that of the violinist; if he takes his violin he can, by playing a single note for some seconds, cause vibrations to build up in a wine glass with the result that the glass will shatter with a surprisingly loud explosion.

The soldiers are one end of our illustration on vibration, and the other end? Let us consider Om. If one can say the words, OM MANI PADME HUM in a certain way and keep on saying that for a few minutes, one can build up a vibration of quite fantastic strength. So remember that names are powerful things, and those who have passed over should not be called unduly, nor should they be called in sorrow or grief, for why should our sorrow be allowed to penalize them and make them suffer? Have they not suffered enough already?

We may wonder why we come to this Earth and suffer death, but the answer is that dying refines one, suffering refines one provided that it be not too much suffering, and again we must remind you that in nearly every case (there are certain special exceptions!) no man or woman is ever called upon to bear greater suffering or sorrow than meets his or her particular need of refining at that moment. You will appreciate this when you think of a woman who can swoon with sorrow. The swoon is merely a safety valve so that she is not overburdened with sorrow, so that nothing happens to injure her.

Often a person who has suffered a great sorrow will be numb with grief. Here again, the numbness is a mercy to the one who is left and to the one who has gone on. Numbness can cause the bereaved to be aware of the loss and so to undergo the refining process, but in being aware of the loss, he or she is not unbearably tormented.

The person who has passed over is protected by the numbness of the bereaved, because if the numbness were not present, perhaps the bereaved, with wailing and lamentations, in full possession of his or her faculties, would cause great stress, great drags on the person who had newly passed over.

In the fullness of time it may be that all of us will be able to communicate with those who have passed over in much the same way as we can now use a telephone to get in touch with those who are in some distant city of the world.

By studying this course conscientiously, by having faith in yourself and in the Greater Powers of this life and of the next life, you, too, should be able to get in touch with those who have passed over. It is possible to do so by telepathy, it is possible to do so by clairvoyance and by automatic writing. In this latter, however, you must keep clear of your own distorted imagination, you must control your imagination so that the message which is written out, apparently subconsciously, does not emanate from your consciousness nor from your subconscious, but comes instead directly from one who has passed over and who can see us although most of us cannot, for the moment, see them. Be of good cheer, be of good faith, for believing you can accomplish miracles. Is it not written that faith can move mountains? It certainly can!

Lesson
Twenty-Six

WE ARE GOING TO set down now what we term "Rules for Right Living." These are completely basic rules, rules which are definitely a "must." To them you should add your own rules. First we will set them down and then we will go over them again examining them more carefully so that we may perhaps have some insight into the reasons behind them. Here they are then:—

1. Do as you would be done by.

2. Do not judge others.

3. Be punctual in all that you do.

4. Do not argue about religion nor scoff at the beliefs of others.

5. Keep to your own religion and show complete tolerance to those who are of the different religion.

6. Refrain from dabbling in magic.

7. Refrain from taking intoxicating drinks, and drugs.

Shall we have a look at these rules in somewhat greater detail? We said, "Do as you would be done by." Well, that is good enough because if you are in possession of your normal faculties, you would not stab yourself in the back, nor would you swindle yourself or overcharge yourself. If you are a normal person, you like to look after yourself as much as possible. You will be living according to the Golden Rule if you look after your neighbor as you would yourself. In other words, do as you would be done by. It helps, it works out. This turning the other cheek business works out with normal people. If some person cannot accept your purity of thought and motive, then after you have suffered in silence two, or, at most, three times, you would be well advised to keep free of that person's presence. In the world beyond this life we cannot meet those who are opposed to us, those with whom we are not in harmony. Unfortunately we have to meet some pretty horrible people while on Earth, but we need not do so from choice but only from sheer necessity. So—do as you would be done by and your character will stand you in good stead, and will be as a shining light to everyone. You will be known as a person who does good, as a person who keeps a promise, so that if you are swindled, the swindler will never get any sympathy. In connection with this, it is good to remember that not even the biggest swindlers can take a single cent away from this life.

We also say, "Do not judge others." You may yet be in a similar position to the person whom you have judged or condemned. You know the circumstances relating to your own affairs, but no one else does, not even the person who is nearest and dearest to you can share the thoughts of your soul. No one, upon this Earth at least, can be completely in harmony with another person. Possibly you are married, possibly you are very happy with your partner, but even so, even in the happiest marriages, sometimes a partner will do something which is completely mystifying to the other. Often it is not even possible to explain another's motives.

"Let the innocent among you be the first to cast a stone." "People in glass houses should not throw stones." These are very good teachings because no one is completely innocent. If people were completely pure, completely innocent, they could not stay on this bad old Earth of ours, so by saying that the innocent only should throw stones, then there is no one to throw stones.

We are, quite bluntly, all in very much of a mess down here on Earth. People come here to learn things, if they had nothing to learn they would not come here, they would go to a better place altogether. We all make mistakes, many of us get blamed for things we have not done, many of us do not get credit for the good which we have done. Does it matter? Later, when we leave this Earth, when we leave our training school, we shall find that the standards are very different indeed, the standards will not be in pounds sterling, nor in dollars, nor pesos or rupees; the standards? We shall then be assessed at our true worth. So, do not judge others.

Our third rule—"Be punctual in all you do," may be rather a surprise to you, but it is a logical rule. People arrange to do things, people have their plans, and there is a time and a place for everything. In being unpunctual, we may upset the plans and ideas of the other person, in being unpunctual we may build up some resentment in the person who has been kept waiting so long, and if we build up resentment and frustration that person may take a different course to that which originally was the one planned. That means that by being unpunctual we have caused another person to take a course of action not originally planned, and that is our responsibility.

Punctuality can be a habit quite as much as can unpunctuality, but punctuality is tidy, it is the disciplining of the body, of the spirit and of the soul, too. Punctuality shows respect for oneself because it means that one is able to keep one's word, and it shows respect for others because in that case we are punctual because we respect others. Punctuality, then, is a virtue which is well worth cultivating. It is a virtue which increases our own mental and spiritual status.

Now about religion; it is wrong indeed to scoff at another person's religion. You believe this, another person believes that. Does it matter what you call God? God is God whatever He is called. Can you argue about the two sides of a coin? Unfortunately throughout the history of mankind there has been too much bad thought about religion—about religion which should cause only good thought.

We repeat to a certain extent this rule about religion in Rule 5, because we say that one should keep to one's own religion. It is rarely wise to change. While upon Earth we are in midstream, the midstream of life, and it is not wise to change horses in mid stream!

Most of us came to this Earth with a certain plan in mind. For most of us that entailed believing in a certain religion or a certain form or branch of religion, and unless there are the strongest of strong reasons it is unwise to change one's religion.

One assimilates religion as one assimilates the language when young. Just as it is always harder to learn a language when one is older, so is it harder to be able to absorb the nuances of a different religion.

It is also wrong to try to influence another person to change to a different religion. What may be suitable for you may not be suitable for the other person. Remember Rule 2, and do not judge others. You cannot judge what religion will suit other people unless you can get inside their skin, get inside their minds, and get inside their souls as well. Lacking the ability to do that, it may be considered an unwise thing indeed to interfere with, to weaken, or to scoff at the religious beliefs of others. Just as we should do as we would be done by, we should give full tolerance, full freedom to other people to believe and worship as they think fit. We would resent interference ourselves, so let us realize that the other person may resent it also.

Rule 6 is, "Refrain from dabbling in magic." That is because many forms of magic are harmful. There are many, many things in occultism which can harm one immensely if one studies without guidance.

An astronomer would never gaze at the Sun through a high-powered telescope without taking suitable precautions, without, in fact, having some suitable sun filters in front of the lens. Even the poorest astronomer would know that gazing upon the Sun through a high-powered telescope would result in blindness. In much the same way, dabbling in the occult without suitable training, without suitable guidance, can lead to nervous breakdown, or can lead to a whole host of thoroughly unpleasant symptoms.

We are definitely opposed to the practice of taking Eastern yogic exercises and trying to torture a poor Western body into some of those postures. These exercises are designed for the Eastern body which has been schooled in these postures from the very earliest days, and it can harm one immensely to get oneself in a contorted mess of bruised muscles just because the exercise has a yogic title. Let us study occultism, by all means, but let us study it sensibly and with guidance.

We do not advise one to "commune with the dead" or do other remarkable practices of that type. It can be done, of course, and is done every day, but it is a matter which can be thoroughly painful and harmful to both sides unless it is done under the competent supervision of a trained teacher.

Some people study the daily newspaper to see what their horoscope is for that day. Many people, unfortunately, take these forecasts absolutely seriously and model their life upon them. Astrological sun-sign forecasts are useless and danger-ous things unless prepared according to exact natal data by a competent astrologer, and the cost of such astrologer's ser-vices would be high indeed because of the considerable knowledge required and the time which the computations would take. It is not enough to judge the Sun sign or Moon sign, or the color of one's hair, or whether one's toes turn up or not; one can do it exactly only if one has the training and the data. So, unless you know of an astrologer who has that training, and patience and the time available, and unless you have an ample supply of money with which to pay for all this time and knowledge, we suggest you do not dabble in astrology. It can cause you harm. Instead study only that which is pure and innocent such as, we venture to say with due modesty, this course which is, after all, but an exposition of natural laws, laws which relate even to breathing and to walking.

Our last rule was, "Refrain from taking intoxicating drinks or drugs." Well, we should have said enough throughout this course to let you realize the dangers of driving the astral body willy-nilly from the physical body, and—as it were—stunning it.

Intoxicating drinks harm the soul, they distort the impres-sions transmitted through the silver cord, they impair the mechanism of the brain which, we must remember, is but a receiving and transmitting station concerned with the manip-ulation of the body upon Earth and the receipt of knowledge in the world beyond.

Drugs are even worse, for drugs are even more habit-forming. If one is going to take to drugs, then one is in effect abandoning all that one aspires to in this life, and in giving way to the false blandishments of intoxicating drinks and drugs, one may be paving the way for life after life upon Earth, until one has thoroughly worked out the karma which that silly, silly habit has built up for us.

All life should be ordered, all life should have discipline. A religious belief, if one adheres to one's belief, is a useful form of spiritual discipline. One sees nowadays teenage gangs in all the cities of the world. Through World War II home ties were weakened; perhaps the father went to the war and the mother worked in a factory, with the result that young, impressionable children played on the streets without any adult supervision, and these young, impressionable children banded together into gangs, they made their own form of discipline, the discipline of gangsterdom. We believe that until the discipline of the love of parents, and the discipline of religion can take over, then teenage crime will continue and increase. If we all have mental discipline, we may be able to set some sort of example to those who have not, for, remember, discipline is essential. It is discipline that distinguishes a highly trained army from a disorganized rabble.

Lesson Twenty-Seven

WE ARE GOING TO bring our old friend, the subconscious, to the forefront because the relationship between the conscious mind and the subconscious mind offers an explanation as to why hypnotism works.

We are really two people in one. One of these people is a little person a ninth the size of the other, an active little person who likes to interfere, likes to be bossy, likes to control. The other person, the subconscious, is likened to an amiable giant without reasoning power, for the conscious mind has reason and logic but no memory, the subconscious mind cannot use reason and has no logic but it is the seat of memory. Everything that has ever happened to a person, even things that happened before birth, are retained within the subconscious, and under suitable types of hypnosis that memory can be released for consideration by others.

One might say—for the purpose of this illustration—that the body as a whole represents a very large library. In the front office, or the the front desk, we have a librarian. Her chief virtue is that while she may not know much about different subjects, she will know instantly the books which contain the desired information. She is adept at consulting filing cards and then producing the book with desired knowledge. People are like that. The conscious mind has this ability to reason (often incorrect reasoning, too) and it is able to exercise a form of logic, but it has no memory. Its virtue is that when trained it can stir up the subconscious so that the latter provides information stored in the memory cells. Between the subconscious mind and the conscious mind, there is what we might call a screen which effectively blocks off all information from the conscious mind. It means that the conscious mind cannot just probe around in the subconscious at any time. This, of course, is absolutely necessary because one would eventually contaminate the other. We stated that the subconscious had memory but no reason. It will be clear that if the memory could be combined with reason, then some facets of information would be distorted because the subconscious, with the power of reasoning, might say in effect, "Oh that is ridiculous! That cannot possibly be! I must have misread the facts, let me alter my memory banks." So it is that the subconscious is without reason, and the conscious is without memory. We have two rules to remember:—

1. The subconscious mind is without reason, therefore it can only act upon suggestion as given to it. It can only retain in the memory any statement true or untrue which is given to it, it is not able to evaluate whether that information is true or false.

2. The conscious mind can only concentrate upon one idea at a time. You will readily appreciate that all the time we

are receiving impressions, forming opinions, seeing things, hearing things and touching things. If the subconscious mind were unprotected, then everything would pour in and we would have our memories cluttered with quite useless information, frequently incorrect information. Between the subconscious and the conscious mind there is a screen that can block off those matters which have to be considered by the conscious before they can be passed on to the subconscious for filing. The conscious mind, then, limited to considering one thought at a time, selects the thought which appears to be the most important, examines the thought, accepts or rejects it in the light of reason or logic.

You may complain that this cannot possibly be so because you personally can think of two or three things at once. But that is not the case; thought is very quick indeed and it is an established fact that thought changes even faster than a lightning flash, so, although you may consciously think that you have two or three thoughts at once, careful investigation by scientists prove that only one thought can occupy the attention at one time.

We should make it clear that, as we have already stated, the memory banks of the subconscious mind hold a knowledge of everything that has ever happened to that particular body. This conscious threshold or screen does not prevent the entry of information, everything pours into the subconscious memory, but information which has to be scrutinized by the logical reasoning brain is held back until such time as it has been evaluated.

Let us see, then, how hypnotism works. The subconscious mind has no power of discrimination, no power of reasoning, no power of logic, so if we can force a suggestion through the screen which normally exists between the conscious and the subconscious, we can cause the subconscious to behave as we want it to! If we concentrate conscious attention upon a single thought, then we increase the suggestibility. If we put the thought to people that they will be hypnotized, and they believe that they will be hypnotized then they will be, because that screen is then lowered. Many people boast that they cannot be hypnotized, but they boast about it rather too volubly. In denying their susceptibility to hypnosis they are merely intensifying their susceptibility, because, again, in any battle between the imagination and the will, the imagination always wins. People may will themselves not to be hypnotized. It is then as though the imagination rises up in wrath and says, "You jolly well will be hypnotized!" And the subjects "go under" almost before they know that anything has happened.

Of course you know how one becomes hypnotized. It will not harm us, though, to go into it again. The best thing to do is to have some method of attracting a person's attention so that the conscious mind, which can hold one thought only at a time, is held captive and then suggestions can creep into the subconscious.

Usually the hypnotist has a bright button or a piece of glass, or some other gimmick, and he asks the subject to consciously focus attention upon that glittering object, and to focus attention unwaveringly upon that object. The whole purpose of this, we repeat, is to so engage the conscious mind that it cannot perceive that certain workings are taking place behind its back!

The hypnotist will hold an object just above eye-level because in looking up to that level a person's eyes are put in an unnatural position of strain. It strains the muscles of the eyes and the eyelids as well, and the eyelid muscles are quite definitely the weakest muscles in the human body, and tire more quickly than does any other muscle.

A few seconds, and the eyes tire, they begin to water. It is a simple matter then for the hypnotist to state that the eyes are tired and that the person wants to sleep. Of course he wants to close his eyes because the hypnotist has just thoroughly tired those muscles! Deadly monotony in repeating that the eyes are tired bores the subject, and knocks down the guard—the awareness—of the subject. Frankly he is thoroughly bored with the whole affair, and feels that he would gladly sleep to have something different to do.

When this has been done a few times, the suggestibility of the subject has been increased, that is, he is forming the habit of becoming hypnotically influenced. So, when a person—the hypnotist—says that the subject's eyes are becoming tired, the subject accepts that without the slightest hesitation because previous experiences have proved that the eyes did become tired under those conditions. Thus, the subject places more and more faith in the statements of the hypnotist.

The subconscious mind is quite uncritical, it is not able to discriminate, so if the conscious mind can accept the proposition that eyes become tired when the hypnotist says so, then the subconscious will also agree that there shall be no pain when the hypnotist says so. In that case, a hypnotist who knows his job can make sure that a woman has completely painless childbirth, or that a patient has a dental extraction without any pain or discomfort. It is a simple matter indeed, and it needs merely slight practice.

The whole thing is, then, that a person who is going to be hypnotized has accepted the statements of the hypnotist. In other words, the subject was told that his eyes were becoming tired. His own experience proved to him that his eyes were becoming tired. He was told by the hypnotist that he would feel much ease if he closed his eyes, and when he did close his eyes he did feel ease.

A hypnotist always has to make sure that his statements are thoroughly believed by the person being hypnotized. It is useless to tell a person that he is standing up when obviously he is lying down. Most hypnotists only tell the subject of a certain thing after the thing has been proved. For instance:—

The hypnotist may tell the subject to stretch out her arm at full length. The hypnotist will repeat it in a monotonous voice for some time, and then when he sees that the subject's arm is becoming tired he will say, "Your arm is becoming tired, your arm is feeling heavy, your arm is becoming tired." The subject can readily agree to that remark because it is self-evident that she is becoming tired, but in the light trance state she is not in a position to say to the hypnotist, "Well, you idiot! Of course it is tired as I am keeping it out like this!" Instead she just believes that the hypnotist has some certain power, some certain ability which can make her do whatever is ordered.

In the future it will be that doctors and surgeons will resort more and more to hypnotic methods, because there is no after-effect with hypnotism, nothing painful, nothing at all disturbing. Hypnotism is natural and almost every person is susceptible to hypnotic commands. The more a person asserts that he or she cannot be hypnotized, the more easy it is to hypnotize that person.

We are not concerned with hypnotizing other people, however, because unless in highly trained hands that can be a highly dangerous and evil thing. We are concerned in helping you to hypnotize yourself, because if you hypnotize yourself, you can get away from bad habits, you can cure yourself of weaknesses, you can raise your temperature in cold weather, and do a lot of useful things like that.

We are not going to teach you how to hypnotize others because we consider it to be dangerous unless one has years of experience. There are certain factors about hypnotism which we are going to mention, though, and in the next lesson we will deal with self- or auto-hypnotism.

It is said in the West that no person can be hypnotized instantly. That is incorrect. Any person can be hypnotized instantly by one who has been trained in certain Eastern methods. Fortunately few Westerners have been so trained.

It is also stated that people cannot be hypnotized and compelled to do a thing in opposition to their own moral code. Here again, this is false, it is absolutely false.

One could not go up to a righteous, good living man, hypnotize him, and say, "Now you go out and rob a bank!" The subject would not do it, he would just wake up instead. But a skillful hypnotist can so phrase his commands and his words that the hypnotized subject believes that he is taking part in a play or in a game.

It is possible, for instance, for a hypnotist to do very wrong things to another person. All he has to do is, by suitably chosen words and suggestions, to persuade the subject that he or she is with perhaps a loved one, a trusted one, or again, is playing. We do not propose to deal any more with this particular aspect of it, because hypnotism is truly a shockingly dangerous thing in unscrupulous hands, and in untrained hands. We suggest that you have nothing whatever to do with hypnotism unless it be treatment under the care of a reputable, highly experienced, highly trained medical practitioner. In dealing with auto- or self-hypnotism, if you follow our instructions you cannot harm yourself and you cannot harm anyone else. On the contrary, you can do a lot of good for yourself and perhaps for other people too.

Lesson
Twenty-Eight

IN THE LAST LESSON, and, indeed, throughout this course, we have seen how we are really two people in one, one being the subconscious and the other being the conscious. It is possible to make one work for the other instead of being as two separate entities almost entirely self-contained and separate. The subconscious entity is the storer of all knowledge, one might say the custodian of the records or the head librarian. The subconscious entity can be likened to a person who never goes out, never does anything except store knowledge and operate things through giving orders to others.

The conscious mind, on the other hand, can be likened to a person of no memory or of very little memory, and of very little training. The person is active, happy, hopping from one thing to another, and only using the subconscious as a means of gaining information. Unfortunately, or otherwise, the subconscious normally is not so accessible for all types of knowledge. Most people, for example, cannot remember the time they were born, yet all that is stored in the subconscious. It is even possible by suitable means to take a hypnotized person back to the time before they were born, and although it is a most interesting experience it is not one that we intend to deal with at length here.

We will tell you, as a matter of interest, that it is possible to hypnotize a person over a series of interviews and to take that person back through successive years of the life so that we go to the time of birth, and to the time beyond birth. We can even take a person to the time when they were planning to come down to the Earth again!

But our purpose in this lesson is to see how we may hypnotize ourselves. It is common knowledge that anyone knows that one person can be hypnotized by another, but in this case we want to hypnotize ourselves, for many people have a distinct aversion to placing themselves at what is quite literally the mercy of another person, because, although in theory a pure, high-minded person cannot harm those being hypnotized, we can claim that except in exceptional circumstances certain transference takes place.

A person who has been hypnotized by another person is always more susceptible to the hypnotic commands of that person. For that reason we personally do not recommend hypnosis. We feel that before it can be perfected for medical use, there should be additional safeguards, for example—no one medical practitioner should be allowed to hypnotize a person, there should always be two medical practitioners present. We would also like to see a law whereby a person who hypnotizes another has himself been hypnotized and a compulsion implanted within so that he cannot do anything which would harm the people he, himself, is going to hypnotize. And we would like the practitioner to undergo hypnosis himself about every three years in order to have that safeguard to patients renewed, otherwise patients are truly at the mercy of the practitioner. Although we would agree that the great, great majority of practitioners are entirely honorable and entirely ethical, one does come across the occasional black sheep who, in this work, is very very black indeed.

Now let us get on with this business of hypnotizing one-self. If you study this lesson properly you will indeed have a key which will enable you to unlock unsuspected powers and abilities within you. If you do not study this properly, then it will just be a meaningless babble of words and you will have wasted your time.

We suggest that you go to your bedroom and pull the curtains to exclude the light, but above your eyes fix a very small light of the night-light type. Extinguish all lights except that one, that light must be so arranged that your eyes look upward slightly—slightly higher than a straight ahead look.

Turn out all the lights except that little neon-glow lamp, and then stretch out as comfortably as possible upon your bed. For a few moments do nothing except breathe as evenly as you can and just let your thoughts wander. Then, after a minute or two of idle thought-wandering, pull yourself to-gether and decide quite firmly that you are going to relax. Tell yourself that you are going to relax every muscle in your body. Think of your toes, dwell upon your toes, it is more convenient to dwell upon the right toe first. Imagine that the whole of your body is a great city, imagine that you have little people occupying every cell of your body. It is these little people who work your muscles and tendons, and who attend to the needs of the cells, that make you tingle with life. But now you want to relax, you do not want all these little people bumbling about distracting you with a twitch here or a twitch there. Concentrate first on your right toes, tell the little people in the right toes to start marching, let them march out of your toes into your foot, up to your instep, along to your ankle. Let them move up the calf of your leg along to the knee.

Behind them, the toes of your right foot will be limp, lifeless, completely relaxed, because there is no one and nothing there to cause feeling—all these little people are marching away, marching up your leg. Your right calf is now quite relaxed, there is no feeling in it; your right leg, in fact, is quite heavy, lifeless, numb, without feeling and so quite relaxed. March the little people all the way up to your right eye and make sure that the policemen on duty there put barriers across the road so that none may slip back. Your right leg, then, from toes to thigh is completely, utterly relaxed. Wait a moment, make sure that it is so, then move to the left leg. Imagine, if you like, that a factory whistle has blown and all the little people are hurrying away from work, leaving their machines, and going home to their leisure. Imagine that they have a good cooked supper ready. Hurry them away from the toes of your left leg, hurry them along up the instep, up the ankle, along the calf into the knee. Behind them the left toes and foot and lower leg will be completely relaxed, completely heavy, as if not belonging to you any more.

Get those people moving, get them up beyond your knee, get them up the thigh. Now, as before in the case of the right leg, in the left leg make your imaginary policemen put barriers so that no one may slip back.

Is your left leg completely relaxed? Make sure. If it is not completely relaxed, order the little people out of the way again so that you are left with the two legs as an empty factory with everyone gone home, with not even maintenance men left there to cause disturbance or noise. Your legs are relaxed. Now do the same with your right hand and arm, and your left hand and arm. Send all the workers away, send them off, get them moving, get them moving like a flock of sheep gets moving in a hurry when a really good sheepdog gets after them. Your purpose is to drive these little people away from your fingers, away from the palm of your hand, away from your wrist, up your forearm, past the elbow—get them moving, clear them out, you want to relax because if you can relax and remain free from all distractions, remain free from all internal buzzes and ticks and clicks, you can unlock your subconscious and then you can be the possessor of powers and knowledge not normally given to ordinary people. You have to play your part, you have to get those little people out of your limbs, get them moving, get them away from your body.

Having got your arms and your legs completely, utterly relaxed, and left like an empty housing estate when everyone has gone off to the local sports match, do the same with your body. Your hips, your back, your stomach, your chest—everything. These little people, they are a nuisance to you. Granted they are necessary to keep life within you, but on this occasion you want them to take a holiday away from you. Well, move them off, march them up along the silver cord, get them away from your body, get yourself free from their irritating influence, then you will be completely and utterly relaxed, and you will know greater ease within you than you have ever thought possible.

With all the little people crowded onto your silver cord, and with your body empty—drained of little people—make sure that you have guardians at the end of the silver cord so that none of these little people may slip back and cause a disturbance.

Take a deep breath, make sure it is a slow, deep, satisfying breath. Hold it for a few seconds, and then release it slowly, taking a few more seconds about it. There should be no strain in this, it should be easy, it should be comfortable, and natural.

Do it again. Take a deep breath, a deep, slow, satisfying breath. Hold it for a few seconds and you will hear your heart going "bump, bump, bump" inside your ears. Then release it, release that breath slowly, slowly, slowly. Tell yourself that your body is completely relaxed, that you feel pleasantly limp and at ease. Tell yourself that every muscle within you is becoming relaxed, your neck muscles are slack, there is no tension within you, there is only ease, comfort and relaxation within you.

Your head is becoming heavy. The muscles in your face trouble you no longer, there is no tension, you are relaxed and comfortable.

Idly contemplate your toes, your knees and your hips. Tell yourself how pleasant it is to feel so relaxed, to feel that there is no tension, to feel that there is nothing pulling or twitching within you. Go higher, feel that there is no tension within your body anywhere, no tension within your arms, within your chest, nor within your head. You are calmly resting fully at ease, and every part, every muscle and every nerve, every tissue within your body is completely and utterly relaxed.

You must be sure that you are completely and utterly relaxed before doing anything further in the matter of self-hypnosis, because it is only the first or second time which will cause you any shadow of trouble. After you have done it once or twice, it will appear to be so natural, so easy, that you will wonder why you have never done it before. Take particular care this first or second time, go slowly at it, there is no need to rush, you have lived all your life so far without it, so a few more hours will not matter. Take it easy, do not strain, do not try too hard, for if you try too hard you will make it easy for doubts and hesitations and muscular fatigue to set in.

If you find that any particular part of your body isn't relaxed, then devote special attention to it. Imagine that you have some particularly conscientious workers in that part of the body, and they want to finish some specific job on hand before leaving at the end of the day. Well, send them off, no job is so important as this upon which you are now engaged.

It is essential that you relax for the good of yourself and for the good of your "workers."

Now, if you are quite sure that you are relaxed in all parts of your body, raise your eyes so that you can see that little neon night-light flickering away somewhere just above your head. Raise your eyes so that there is a slight strain on the eyes and on the eyelids as you gaze at the light. Now keep looking at that night-light. Its a nice, pleasant little reddish glow, it should make you feel drowsy. Tell yourself that you want to get your eyelids to close when you have counted ten, so count: "One, two, three, my eyes are becoming tired—four, yes, I am becoming drowsy—five, I can hardly keep my eyes open. . . ," and so on until you get to nine. "Nine, my eyes are closing tightly—ten, my eyes will stay open no longer, they are shut."

The point of this is that you want to set up a definite conditioned reflex so that in future auto-hypnotic sessions you will have no difficulty at all, you will not have to waste time with all this relaxing, all you will have to do is to count, and then you will go off to sleep into the hypnotic state, and that is the aim which you now seek to attain.

Now certain people may have a few doubts, and their eyes will not close the first time at the count of ten. There is no need to worry about this, because if your eyes will not close willingly, then close them deliberately as though you were in fact in the hypnotic state. If you do this deliberately, you will be laying a foundation for that conditioned reflex, and that is a thing which is quite essential.

Again, you want to say something like this, the actual words do not matter, this is just to give you some idea with which you can make your own formula.

"When I have counted up to ten my eyelids will become very, very heavy and my eyes will become tired. I will have to close my eyes, and nothing will keep them open after I have reached the count of ten. The moment I do let my eyes close I shall fall into a state of complete self-hypnosis. I shall be fully conscious, and I shall hear and know everything that happens, and I shall be able to order my subconscious mind as I want to."

Then you count as we told you before, "One, two, my eyelids are becoming very heavy, my eyes are becoming tired—three, I have difficulty in keeping my eyes open—nine, I cannot keep my eyes open—ten, my eyes are closed and I am in a self-hypnotic state."

We feel that we should end this lesson here because it is such an important lesson. We want to end it here so that you may have ample time to practice. If we gave more in this lesson, you might be inclined to read too much at one time, and to take in too little at one time. So, will you study this again and again? We assure you repeatedly that if you will study, if you will assimilate this and practice this, you will have truly wonderful results.

Lesson
Twenty-Nine

IN OUR LAST LESSON we dealt with the method of getting ourselves into the trance stage. Now we have to practice that several times. We can make it much easier for ourselves if we really practice, so that we can get into the trance stage easily without having to make hard labor of it, because the whole point of this is to save you hard labor.

Let us also look at the reason for this; you want to hypnotize yourself so that you may eliminate certain faults, so that you may strengthen certain virtues, certain abilities. Now what are those faults? What are those abilities? You must be able to focus the faults and the virtues clearly. You have to be able to really conjure up a picture of yourself as you want to be. Are you weak-willed? Then picture yourself exactly as you want yourself to be, with a strong will and a dominant personality, able to get over your points, able to sway men and women in the way that you want to sway them.

Keep on thinking of this "new you." Keep the picture of this "you" steadily before you in much the same way as an actor—a star—actually lives the part he is going to play. You must use your full powers of visualization; the more firmly you can visualize yourself as you want to be, then the more quickly you can attain your objective. Keep on practicing, putting yourself in a trance, but always make sure that you are practicing in a quiet, darkened room. There is no danger in any of this. We stress that you should make sure that you are not interrupted because any interruption, or any draft of cold air for instance, will cause you to wake up, cause you to snap out of that trance in a hurry. There is no danger, we repeat, it is definitely not possible for you to hypnotize yourself and fail to come out of the trance. To reassure you, let us take a typical case. The patient has had a lot of practice. He goes to his darkened room, switches on the little neon light just above the eyebrow level, and composes himself comfortably upon his bed or couch. For some moments he works at getting the body relaxed, free from stresses and strains.

Soon he feels a wonderful sensation stealing over him as if all the weight of the body, all the cares of the body are dropping off, and he is about to enter a new life. He relaxes more and more, leisurely reaching out with his mind to see if there is any muscle under tension, to see if there is any twitch, any ache, any strain anywhere. Satisfied that he is completely relaxed, he gazes steadily at the little neon light, his eyes are not pointed straight ahead, but are inclined upward somewhat toward his eyebrows.

Soon his eyelids begin to feel heavy, they flutter a little and then close, but only for a second or two. They flutter open again, there is some moisture, his eyes are watering. They flutter and tremble, they close again. Once more they open, with difficulty this time, for the eyes are tired, the lids are heavy, and the person is almost in deep trance. Within a second or so, the lids close, and this time they stay tightly closed. The body relaxes even more, the breathing becomes shallow, the patient—the subject, call him what you will—is in the trance stage.

Now let us leave him for a moment. What he is doing in that trance is no concern of ours because we can go into a trance ourselves and have our own experiences. Let us leave him in the trance stage until he has completed that for which he went into the trance.

He was doing an experiment, it seems, to see how deeply he could hypnotize himself, to see how firmly he could stay asleep. He deliberately tried to set aside one of the provisions of nature because he told himself he was not going to wake up!

Minutes—ten minutes, twenty minutes?—pass. The breathing changes and the subject is no longer in a trance, but is sound asleep. After half an hour or so, he awakens feeling wondrously refreshed, more refreshed, indeed, than after a complete night's sleep. You cannot fail to awaken out of a trance, nature will not allow it. The subconscious is like a rather dim giant—a giant with dim intellect—for a time you can persuade him anything you like, but after a time it dawns upon this dim giant that he is "having his leg pulled." Then he snaps out of the hypnotic state. We repeat again that you cannot put yourself to sleep in any way which would cause you harm or even discomfort. You are utterly safe, because you will have hypnotized yourself and not be at the mercy of any other person's suggestions.

We said before that a draft of cold air would awaken a person; that is so. No matter how deep the trance, if there is a change of temperature, or anything that might possibly in any way whatever harm the body, the trance passes. So it is that if you are in a trance and someone in the house opens a door or a window so that a draft of air comes to you, perhaps under the door or through the keyhole, you will be awakened safely, painlessly, and then you will have the trouble of starting all over again. That is why you should avoid drafts and disturbances.

At all times you will have to stress the virtues that you want to acquire. You will have to stress that you are getting rid of the things that you do not admire, and for some days as you walk about, you will have to actively visualize the abilities which you want. You will tell yourself time after time throughout the day that at such-and-such a time—preferably that night—you are going to hypnotize yourself, and each time you go into a trance the desired virtues will appear more strongly in you. As you go into your trance, repeat within your mind that which you desire.

Just a simple, perhaps silly little illustration—let us say that a man stoops, perhaps because he is too lazy to stand upright. Let him say repeatedly, "I will stand upright—I will stand upright—I will stand upright." The point is, again, that you must repeat this quickly time after time with no break in between, because if you do permit a break, Friend Subconscious might come in and say, "Oh, you never tell the truth, you stoop like anything!" If you repeat it without giving a break, Friend Subconscious hasn't a chance, he becomes overwhelmed by the weight of words and soon believes that you stand up straight. If he does believe that, your muscles will tighten and you will stand straight just as you want.

Do you smoke too much? Drink too much? It's bad for the health if carried to excess, you know! Why not use hypnotism to cure yourself, to save your pocketbook from the constant depletion of what are, after all, rather childish habits. You have only to convince your subconscious that you dislike smoking, and you will stop smoking without a single pang, without a single thought of smoking.

People cannot give up smoking, it is a habit which is extremely hard to break. No doubt you have heard that time after time; a smoker cannot give up his pipe or cigarette, everyone tells you so, advertisements in the paper bring to your attention various so-called remedies for stopping smoking, stopping this, or stopping that. Does it not occur to you that all this is in itself a form of hypnosis? You cannot stop smoking because you believe what you have been told by other people and by the advertisements to the effect that to stop smoking is almost impossible.

Turn that hypnotism to your own use; YOU are different from the common herd, you have a strong character, you are dominant, you can cure yourself of smoking, or drinking, or whatever it is you desire to cure. Just as hypnotism—unconscious hypnotism—made you believe that you could not break the smoking habit, so, when you are aware of this, your conscious hypnotism can make it so that you never touch another cigarette.

A word of warning, though, or might it even be called friendly advice. Are you sure you want to give up smoking? Are you sure you want to give up drinking or always being late for appointments? You cannot do anything until you are sure, you must be certain that you want to give up smoking, that you want to do this or do that. It is not enough to be a very weak man and say, "Oh, I wish I could give up smoking, let me tell myself that I will."

Again and again until it sinks into your subconscious—you can only do that which you really want to do, so that if you more or less dare yourself not to give up smoking, then you will not give up smoking, you might even smoke more!

Examine yourself closely. What do you want to do really? There is no one about, no one looking over your shoulder, no one peering into your mind. Do you really want to give up smoking? Or do you prefer to go on smoking, and is your statement that you want to give up just so many wasted words?

Once you are completely convinced that you do want a thing, you can have it. Do not blame hypnotism, or anything but yourself, if you fail to get what you want, because if you do fail then it means this, and this only: failure means that you were not really strong in your resolution to do this or not do that.

By self-hypnosis you can cure yourself of those things which some people refer to as bad habits. Unfortunately we have never been able to discover what these bad habits were, so we can shed no more light on that particular subject. We will consider bad habits to include baiting your wife or throwing the iron at your husband or kicking the dog, swearing at someone without reason, or getting drunk, and all these things can be cured so very easily provided one definitely wants to.

Let yourself relax a few times. Take advantage of freedom from inner tension to build up your own nervous energy. You can do so much to improve your health if you will only read, and reread this lesson and the one before, and practice, practice, practice. Even the greatest musicians practice scales and notes hour after hour, day after day. That is why they are great musicians. You can be a great self-hypnotist if you do as we say. So, practice.

Lesson
Thirty

MANY PEOPLE HAVE the idea—a most mistaken idea—that there is something wrong with work. Many civilizations are divided into "white collar workers" and those who "get their hands dirty." It is a form of snobbery which should be eradicated because it turns brother against brother and race against race.

Work, no matter whether it be brain work or manual work, is ennobling to those who do it with a clear conscience and without a mistaken sense of shame. In some countries it is considered to be a disgrace if the lady of the house lifts her hand to do any form of work; it is thought that she should sit about and look pretty, and perhaps give a few orders now and then to show that she is the lady of the house!

In old China in days long gone, the upper classes—so-called—grew their fingernails ridiculously long, so long, in fact, that often they would have special sheaths to protect the nails from accidental breakage. The purpose of the long nails was to show that these people were so wealthy that they did not have to do anything at all for themselves; the long nails were proof positive of the inability to work because the lady or gentleman of the house—the wearer of the long nails—could not even attend to his or her bodily needs, and had to have servants to do everything for them.

In Tibet before the Communist invasion certain of the noblemen (who should have known better) wore sleeves so long that they completely covered the hands and dangled perhaps six or twelve inches below the fingertips. This was to show that these men were so important, and so wealthy, that they did not have to work. The long, long sleeves were a constant reminder that they could not work. This, of course, was a degradation of the real purpose of work. Work is a form of discipline, a form of training. Discipline is utterly necessary, it is discipline which makes the difference between a crack regiment of soldiers and a disorganized rabble; it is discipline in the home which makes it possible for youngsters—teenagers—to be decent citizens when they are no longer teenagers—lack of discipline makes for hordes of young people who are bent only on destruction.

We mentioned Tibet as being one of the places where there were wrong ideas about work, but that is only among laymen. In the lamaseries it was a rule that everyone, no matter how exalted, had to do menial work at certain stated times. It was (before the Communist invasion) not an unusual sight to see a High Abbot cleaning a floor—cleaning up rubbish deposited on the floor by the lowest of monks. The purpose of this was to teach the Abbot that things upon the Earth were things of a temporal nature, and the beggar of today might be the prince of tomorrow and the prince of today might be a beggar tomorrow. Some point might possibly be drawn from the fact that many of the crowned heads of Europe and elsewhere are no longer kings and queens and princes ruling countries, but then one has to reflect that many of these former crowned heads and presidents have made very sure while they were still in power that they would have ample funds for when they were no longer in power. However, that is a digression, let us state again that work, no matter what kind of work, whether menial or mental, is uplifting, and never degrading when it is done with pure motives, and with the idea of service to others behind it. Instead of applauding those gilded ladies who sit and autocratically dictate to ill paid servants while not lifting a finger themselves, we should applaud the servants and look down upon the gilded ladies, for the servants are doing something honorable; the gilded ladies are not.

We heard a discussion quite recently—a somewhat heated one—about meat eating. Our own point of view is that if people want to eat meat, then let them eat meat, if people want to be vegetarians and climb trees after nuts, then let them be vegetarians and climb trees after nuts. It does not matter what we eat or do not eat so long as we do not inflict our often erroneous opinions upon others, who may be too polite to object violently.

We are animals, no matter how much we disguise the fact with fine clothes and beautiful facial powders and hair dyes, etc. Not only are we animals, we are meat eating animals, too. In fact, the flesh of mankind tastes, according to all reports, something like pork! Many people behave in a rather piggish manner, so possibly that is quite appropriate. Cannibals, when asked about human flesh, say that the black man's flesh is rather sweet and like roast pork. The white man's flesh is apparently a rather rancid and sour affair, like bad meat.

We suggest, then, that if you want to eat meat, do so. If you want to eat vegetables or grass, do so. But do not at any time inflict your own opinions on others. It is a sad fact that those who are vegetarians or health food addicts are often extreme in their views, as if by the very vehemence of their argument they will convince themselves. It seems to us very decidedly that many of these people whom we personally regard as cranks are uncertain that they are doing the right thing. They do not want to miss anything, but they do not want to be vegetarians themselves if they think that other people are enjoying meat. It is often the case with nonsmokers; nonsmokers often resent greatly that another person shall smoke, they seem to think that there is something exceedingly virtuous in not smoking. Actually it is just a matter of choice. Smoking, in moderation, probably never hurt anyone, but drink—intoxicating liquors—does harm people because it interferes with their astral. We say in connection with this that, again, if people want to drink and injure the astral body, well, that is their choice. It is definitely wrong to try to use any forceful persuasion to change the path of another person.

While we are on the subject of eating meat—which entails killing—let us mention another point which you may find of interest. Some people say that one should never kill even an insect. They say one should never kill a cow or a horse, or anything else which has life in it. It makes us wonder if we are doing a grave ill when we kill a mosquito which threatens to infect us with malaria; it makes us wonder if we are doing a crime against the living world if we have an injection against any virus. After all, a microbe or a virus is a living organism, should we, then, out of our sense of righteousness, stop trying to kill TB germs, stop trying to kill cancer germs? Are we great sinners in trying to find a cure for the common cold? In trying to cure any illness surely we are taking life. We have to be reasonable about all this.

The vegetarians say that we should not take life. Now, a cabbage has life, so if we tear a cabbage from the ground in order that we may eat it, we are destroying life which we cannot create. If we take a potato or a stick of celery, or anything else, we are destroying life, and as the vegetarian destroys life quite as much as the meat eater, why not let us be sensible and eat as the body needs—meat.

It is often stated that the good Buddhist does not eat meat, and we must hasten to agree that many Buddhists do not eat meat and often the reason is that they cannot afford it! Buddhism nourished exceedingly in very, very poor countries. In Tibet, for instance, meat was an unheard of luxury which could be enjoyed only by the richest of the rich. The ordinary people had vegetables and tsampa, the vegetables, too, were a luxury. The monk, who was not addicted to luxury, lived on tsampa and nothing else, but to make it taste better the leaders of the religion decreed that it was wrong to eat meat. Thus, people who could not get meat anyhow felt that they were being virtuous in not having meat. We feel that there is much nonsense written about all these things. The meat eaters like to have meat—well let them. If vegetarians want to chew sticks of celery, let them have celery as long as they do not inflict their views on others. In the same way, if people do not want to kill an insect, and prefer to have their cancer virus or TB germs instead of trying to get cured—that is their choice.

We often get letters from people in great distress who tell us that such-and-such a person is desperately in need of help, of advice, and how can they hypnotize a person, or force a person to a different way of life. We never help in such cases, because we believe that it is indeed very, very wrong to try to influence the path of another person. In this course, for instance, knowledge is available. We state our opinions, we state what we know, but we do not try to force you to believe. If you are taking this course then presumably you are prepared to listen to what we have to say; if you do not want to listen to us it is an easy matter to close the book.

If you are asked to give an opinion, give it, but do not try to force your opinion on other people, and, having given your opinion, let the whole matter drop because you do not know what others arranged as their path through life. If you are going to force people to do something which they do not want to do, then you might be fixed with their karma. It might be an unpleasant karma, too!

We want to say something here about animals; many people regard animals merely as creatures who walk about on four legs instead of on two. People regard animals as dumb creatures because they do not speak English, French, German, or Spanish, but then animals regard humans as dumb creatures also! If you were truly telepathic, you would find that animals do talk, and they talk far more intelligently than many humans! Some scientists, have discovered that there is a language of bees. Bees can give very detailed instructions to each other, and they even hold conferences.

Some scientists became interested in dolphins, in their peculiar speech, or, as they thought of it, in the peculiar sounds which they made. These sounds were recorded on a tape recorder, and were then reproduced at different speeds. At one speed the speech sounded very, very much like human speech.

Animals are entities which have come down to this Earth in a special shape, in a special form, in order that they may do their own task in a manner most suitable for their own evolution. We are in the fortunate position of having been associated with two Siamese cats who were quite phenomenally telepathic, and with these—after much experience—it is possible to carry out conversation in much the same way as one can with intelligent humans. Sometimes it is not at all flattering to pick up the thoughts of how a Siamese cat regards a human. If we regard animals as our equals who are in a different physical form, we can get very close to them, we can discuss with them things which otherwise would be impossible.

A dog, for instance, likes the friendship of people. A dog likes to be subservient because then he gets praise and flattery.

A Siamese cat, on the other hand, often has quite a contempt for humans, because a human compared to a Siamese cat is a very handicapped person indeed, a Siamese cat has remarkable occult powers and remarkable telepathic powers. So, why not get on good terms with your own cat, or your dog, or your horse? If you want to, if you sincerely believe, then you can with practice converse by telepathy with that animal.

So we come to the end of this course, but, we hope, not the end of our association. This course is a practical course which we trust has shown you how absolutely ordinary, how absolutely simple, all these so-called metaphysical phenomena really are. We have another course which deals with the subjects in the more traditional style, giving you Sanskrit names, etc. We suggest that it is very much to your advantage to consider this course, because now that you have studied this far with us, assuredly you will want to go further.

We will not say, "Goodbye," then, because we hope that you will join us for a little longer. Let us say instead in Spanish "Hasta la Vista."